The Millionaire Factory

A Complete System for Becoming Insanely Rich

Andrii Sedniev

The Millionaire Factory

A Complete System for Becoming Insanely Rich

Published by Andrii Sedniev

Copyright © 2019 by Andrii Sedniev

ISBN 978-1-09671-818-5

First printing, 2019

www.AndriiSedniev.com

PRINTED IN THE UNITED STATES OF AMERICA

Dedications

This book and my love are dedicated to Olena, my wife and partner, who makes every day in life worthwhile. Thank you for supporting me in every stage of development of *The Millionaire Factory* system and giving encouragement when I needed it the most. Without you, this book might never have been finished.

I also want to dedicate this book to all past students of the *The Millionaire Factory* system who, by their success, inspire me to become a better person every day.

Contents

The Wealth Formula

Several years ago I received a call from my friend Jason, who is not only a serial entrepreneur, but also a billionaire and the wisest man I know. He said: "Andrii, come to my house in Hampton NY with your wife for this weekend. I know that you are working on a book about how to become a millionaire. We will celebrate my school friend Adam becoming a millionaire recently and will have an interesting conversation about how to become insanely rich. I am sure you might pick up an idea or two from either me or Adam. We will also tan at the beach, play some golf and table foosball, it will be really fun."

I said: "It's a long time since we got together, we miss you and your wife, Jane. Of course we will come."

When my wife, Olena, and I arrived at Jason's magnificent mansion we were met by a butler in front of the gate and he walked us inside. Jason said: "You guys arrived just on time, lunch is almost ready." Jason introduced Adam to us: "Andrii, Olena, this is Adam. He is my best school friend and today we are celebrating him gaining his first million dollars in his savings account. Adam works as a chef in New York and you will be able to evaluate his cooking skills…" He looked at his watch: "In about 10 minutes."

During the lunch we were served salads, main course and dessert that were cooked under Adam's supervision. The food not only looked beautiful but it was perhaps the most delicious food that I have ever eaten. Adam's cooking skills impressed me, but the story of how he became rich impressed me even more.

After lunch when Jason, Adam and I were hanging out on the terrace Jason said: "Adam, share with Andrii the story of how you became rich."

Adam smiled and said: "Before I worked as a chef I managed hundreds of millions of equity on Wall Street. I wore expensive suits, I drove a Porsche, I lived in a penthouse, I earned more than one million dollars per year and I was poor."

I asked: "Are you kidding me? You lived in a penthouse, drove a Porsche and you say to me that you were poor?"

Adam said: "Yes, I was poor because I lived according to a poor people's formula which says: you spend everything you have earned. Although I earned a lot I spent a lot and after over 15 years of very high income I had zero in my savings account. So although I lived in a penthouse, at the end of the day I wasn't any wealthier than a homeless bum. The majority of people think that a wealthy person is a person who earns a lot, in fact a wealthy person is a person who spends less than he or she earns."

I asked, "Sounds interesting, but why did you stop working on Wall Street and begin working as a chef?"

Adam continued his story: "One day I had a heart attack because of the insane working hours and stress associated with my work and a doctor recommended that I change careers if I wanted to stay alive. After this incident I decided to start my life over from scratch and to become a chef in a small restaurant to which Jason had recommended me. Since childhood I loved cooking, it was truly my vocation, but I ignored it because I thought that I couldn't make a lot of money with it. During the last seven years I became significantly happier, I feel how my work is appreciated by thousands of people and I earn in interest on my savings more than my salary. Although I work at an ordinary job I am much richer than when I worked at a very well-paid job and the reason for this is The Wealth Formula which Jason has taught me."

After Adam shared his story Jason said: "It's getting a bit chilly here. Let's get our women and go for a walk on the beach. It would be also a great place to talk about The Wealth Formula. Although this formula is very simple, I never get tired of reminding it to myself and others because it's the single most precious piece of knowledge that I have."

After we went out to the beach in front of Jason's house and started walking along the coast of the Atlantic Ocean he continued: "The Wealth Formula says: (Income − Cost of Living)*(Interest on Investment) = Growing Wealth. Poor people save money in order to spend it and wealthy people save money in order to invest it and make even more money. Many people think that you become rich because of earned money, but in reality you become rich because of correctly invested saved money. Rich people know that no matter how talented and productive you are, you can produce a very limited amount of value with your own labor. In order to significantly increase the amount of value you generate, you need to make your money work for you and in this case the amount of value that you can create will be unlimited. In order to activate The Wealth Formula you need to learn how to do just three things: maximize your primary source of income, reduce your cost of living, invest money with the highest interest and the lowest risk. Rich people know that it is lonely and ineffective to work alone, so they make their partner, by the name of Money, work hard with them. Although this formula is extremely simple, the majority of people ignore it and stay poor forever, however those who follow it inevitably become rich."

We walked for about five more minutes in silence enjoying a beautiful sunset and Jason continued: "Here is an exact strategy for how you can become insanely rich by using The Wealth Formula. First you need to increase your primary income that you earn through a salary or business. In order to do so you need to do work that you are passionate about, that utilizes your core talents and that brings a lot of value to others. Second, to increase the amount of money that you save, you need to limit your spending until you become rich and are able to live on less than 25% of your yearly income. Finally in order to get a maximum return on your money, you need to invest this difference with the highest return and the lowest risk. Whenever you can, you should invest into your primary source of income such as your business or career growth because it's something you understand, it's something you have a talent for, something that you are passionate about and usually brings the highest return on investment with the lowest risk. After that, invest the remaining savings into an S&P 500 Index fund that represents the entire USA market that can give you approximately 10% per year with second-best risk after the first option. Finally run all purchases that you make through a credit card with cash back that will allow you to gain an additional 2% on your money without any risk at all. Once I realized that there exist only three good options with which you can gain return on your money, I freed my mind and was able to dedicate my entire attention to developing my primary source of income and maximizing the amount of value that I create for the world through my vocation, and it boosted enormously the rate at which I accumulate wealth. If somebody had shared with me when I was younger what I have just shared with you, I would have been happy to pay this person any amount of money because I know that this knowledge is worth a fortune and would have saved me many years on the way to becoming rich."

Based on ideas I learned from Jason, Adam and 10 years of my own research of billionaires, entrepreneurs, investors and highly paid employees, I created The Millionaire Factory system. This system provides an effective process of how to become rich for people with any talent, character or occupation. You will learn very specific tips of what to do to maximize your income, how to save like a rich person, where exactly to invest your money, backed up by research and real-life examples. This system proved to be effective for thousands of people around the world and if you follow the recommendations in this book I promise that you will wonder how short the path towards being wealthy or incredibly wealthy will become for you. Are you ready for the trip through the adventurous world of Money? Let's go.

The Millionaire's Triangle

In order to become rich you need to make your income as high as possible and after that make your saved money work for you. In order to make both your income and level of happiness as high as possible you need to devote most of your time to work that adheres to the following 3 criteria: It's something that brings a lot of value to people, it's something that you are passionate about and it's something that utilizes your true talents. I call this intersection The Millionaire's Triangle. Although this concept is simple, it may have an enormous impact on your life and if what you do every day isn't in The Millionaire's Triangle it may cost you a fortune. The Millionaire's Triangle could give you the highest return on time investment and often increases results of your work not twice, not thrice but by hundreds of times. The Millionaire's Triangle is one of the most important concepts not only in the process of becoming rich, but also in the process of becoming happy and fulfilled.

Give value to people

When I was 4 years old one boy by the name of Max in my kindergarten had a birthday and brought a bag of candies to give away to other children. He approached me and said: "Andrii, here is a candy for you." I said: "Thank you, Max." Next he approached a girl sitting next to me, gave her a candy and she said: "Thank you." After that he gave a candy to the rest of the group and everybody said, "Thank you" to him. Why did each of us say, "Thank you" to Max? Because he gave us value, he gave us a candy that we could eat and thereby experience pleasure.

Look at the world around you, in this world the way for people to say "Thank you" for the value that you create for them is to pay money. The more value you create for people, the bigger the "Thank you" they say by paying more money for your work, product or service. The amount of money that you earn every month is exactly how much value you create for other people in the world. If you want to earn more money, you simply need to create more value for more people so that the overall value that you create for the world is bigger.

Have you ever noticed that the majority of people can't speak well in public? After having analyzed thousands of public speakers around the world I realized that there is one factor that has the highest impact on the success of their speeches and it's intention. If you come on stage with intention to get applause from the audience members, to sell a product or to make others think highly of you, your presentation will fail. People can read nonverbal signals of a speaker and will realize that you care only about yourself and don't care about them. If you don't care about them, they will not care about you and your speech will not achieve the goals that you set for yourself. The best speakers come on stage intending to give as much value to their audience members as possible and to change their lives for the better. When you have such intentions the audience members will realize that you care about them and as a result they will enjoy your speech, they will accept your messages and as a side benefit they will applaud you, will buy your product and will think highly of you.

Money is a measure of value that you create for people, and the same principle as in public speaking works extremely well in a business or career. If your intention is to make a lot of money and spend it on a luxurious life, your customers or employer will sense that you don't care about them and you won't be successful in accumulating wealth. However, if you want to make a lot of money but shift your focus from making money for yourself to bringing as much value as possible for your customers or employer, they will sense that you care about them, and accumulating wealth will become significantly easier.

Think about how much you earn per month right now – it's exactly the amount of value you created. If you want to earn more money you need to focus on creating more value for the world, and as you see from the example above, focusing on creating more value is more effective than focusing on making more money. If you want to become wealthy, create the following intention in your head: "My goal is to create as much value as possible and for as many people as possible. After the value I create is huge, a thank-you from the world in the form of money will come as a side benefit. When I focus on the amount of value that I create for the world I will accumulate significantly more wealth than if I focus on money."

Make it a habit to ask: "How can I bring even more value to other people?" This question will make your brain regularly think about ideas that will improve the lives of others, increase the amount of value that you create for the world and as a side benefit, increase your wealth. In order to make the car go, you first need to fill the tank with gas, in order to make the world send money your way you first need to fill it with value for other people. Think how you can apply your talents and passion to create the most value for other people, so that they can highly appreciate your work. The intention for making the lives of others better not only positively affects your income but also improves your feeling of happiness and sense of fulfillment.

No man can become rich without himself enriching others. — Andrew Carnegie

The person who starts simply with the idea of getting rich won't succeed, you must have a larger ambition — John D. Rockefeller

Writing isn't about making money, getting famous, getting dates, getting laid, or making friends. In the end, it's about enriching the lives of those who will read your work, and enriching your own life, as well. — Stephen King

Do what you are passionate about

Between 1960 and 1980 a psychologist, Dr. Srully Blotnick, conducted research based on 1500 business school graduates. He grouped them into two categories. Category A said they would pursue money first and would do what they are passionate about later in life. This category consisted of 1245 people which represented 83% of all graduates. Category B said that they would focus on their passion and trust that money would follow. This category consisted of 255 people, which represented 17% of all graduates. Twenty years later there were 101 millionaires out of the original group of 1500 people. What startled Dr. Srully Blotnick was that only 1 millionaire was from Category A (follow money) and 100 millionaires were from Category B (follow your passion). If you were one of the graduates in this study who consciously decided to build life around what you are passionate about, your chances for becoming a millionaire would be 488 times higher than if you built life around a desire to become rich.

For several years I have watched thousands of interviews with rich entrepreneurs, employees and self-employed people. All of them were asked how to become successful and how they were able to accumulate impressive wealth starting from scratch. After watching dozens of interviews I learned some interesting ideas, after watching hundreds of interviews I began noticing patterns among these ideas, after watching thousands I realized what one single thing differentiated all these people from others. Although all these wealthy people came from different backgrounds, worked in different industries and had different talents, there was one piece of advice that popped up in every single interview: "Do what you are passionate about. Passion provides you an unlimited amount of energy to work towards your goal." Wealthy people instinctively understand that the impact of passion is enormous and is perhaps the most important factor on the way to success. If you heard this advice as many times as I did, you would realize that working only on things that you are passionate about isn't just blah-blah-blah talk from people who made it, but a key to building a fortune. As you can see from the experiment of Dr. Srully Blotnick, if you work on what you are passionate about your chances for success increase not two times, not even ten times, but sometimes as much as 488 times. If on one side of the scale you put your education, experience, and skills, and on the other side your passion for work, the passion side will outweigh significantly in its impact on success.

In July 2006 when Facebook was only 2 years old, was making only $30 million in revenue and wasn't even profitable, founder Mark Zuckerberg received an acquisition offer from Yahoo for $1 billion. During a three-person board meeting that 22-year-old Mark conducted with Facebook investors Peter Thiel and Jim Breyer he said: "This is kind of a formality, just a quick board meeting, it shouldn't take more than 10 minutes. We're obviously not going to sell here." Peter Thiel said: "We should probably talk about this. A billion dollars is a lot of money." Jim Breyer added: "You own 25 percent. There's so much you could do with the money." Mark thought for a second and said: "I don't know what I could do with the money. I'd just start another social networking site. I kind of like the one I already have." Ten years after this conversation Facebook was worth $500B and Mark Zuckerberg was one of the richest people in the world.

There are 3 questions that you can ask yourself to figure out what you are passionate about: "What is a job that I enjoy doing so much that I would do it on Sunday even if I wasn't paid for it?" "What work gives me the biggest sense of pride and satisfaction?" "What work I could do for 8 hours straight without noticing how the time passed?" The answer to these 3 questions is work that you are passionate about and to which you need to devote your entire life. If your primary motivation for work is money – then you are in the wrong job for becoming rich. If your primary motivation for work is passion and you feel the internal need to do this work as much as you need to breathe, then you are on the fast track to wealth. Most poor people think that work is for making money and you should have fun after work doing something that you enjoy. Rich people know that fun and work should be the same thing and the right way to make big money is to find your vocation and to spend your life around what you are passionate about.

According to Gallup's 2013 report called "State of the American Workplace" that surveyed over 150,000 workers, 70% of people either hate their jobs or are actively disengaged. If you look at your past, you will see that no amount of willpower will force you to do well what you don't like, however if you are passionate about something you will do it with full commitment for an unlimited amount of hours without noticing how the time passed. If you live in resonance with your vocation, you will become an expert in your work, your effort will bring the highest results, you will bring more and more value to people and as a result money will come. If you want to earn a lot of money, you need to make big progress in your work, in order to make big progress in your work you need to spend a lot of energy and the single unlimited source of energy that you have is passion. Without passion, no matter what productivity techniques you use, overcoming laziness and achieving great results is close to impossible.

An interviewer once asked 29-year-old boxing world champion and double Olympic gold medalist Vasil Lomachenko: "Vasil, you have trained in a boxing gym for countless hours since you were 6. How long do you want your professional career to last?" Vasil looked at him and said: "I will do boxing while I enjoy it. The moment I feel that I don't enjoy boxing anymore I will end my professional career." If you consistently experience laziness for the work you do, maybe you shouldn't do this work at all and instead focus on different work that you have a passion for. Don't think that your only option in life is to work on a job for which you obtained education or for which you have years of experience under your belt. If you find that you have stopped enjoying your job, ignore the sunk costs that you experienced related to it and switch to the job you are really passionate about. You can either have half of your career boring and unsuccessful and a second half interesting and successful or the entire career boring and unsuccessful. It's never too late to increase your chances of becoming happy and wealthy 488 times.

The first step to becoming insanely rich is to clearly identify what work you are passionate about and want to dedicate your entire life to. When you begin doing not what your friend, teacher, parent or wife wants you to do, but what you want to do, you will create so much value for society that it will send generous amounts of money your way to say "Thanks." Whatever work you are doing, you are competing with people who love what they do and if you work without passion you don't stand a chance in this competition. Motivation for work has an enormous impact on your chances for earning a lot of money, that's why instead of looking for the most lucrative career path, simply identify what you are passionate about and build your career around it. Passion is the number one reason why people become successful and wealthy, lack of passion is the number one reason why people fail and stay poor.

The only way to do great work is to love what you do. – Steve Jobs

The biggest mistake people make in life is not trying to make a living at doing what they most enjoy. – Malcolm Forbes

You know you are on the road to success if you would do your job, and not be paid for it. – Oprah Winfrey

If you're interested in "balancing" work and pleasure, stop trying to balance them. Instead make your work more pleasurable. – Donald Trump

If you love what you do so much that you are willing to continue to live like a student in order to be able to stay in the job, you have found your calling. – Mark Cuban

Do what you have talent for

My friend Julia wanted to have children and when the doctor said: "Congratulations! You are going to have twins," she and her husband were in seventh heaven. When her sons Mark and Vlad turned 7, Julia signed them up for singing and acrobatics classes. Julia said to me during our conversation over a cup of coffee: "After a year I began realizing how different my children are. Mark enjoyed singing classes, had the best progress in the group and received praise from his teacher. Vlad hated singing classes and didn't make any progress no matter how much effort he applied. With acrobatics classes the situation was completely the opposite. Vlad enjoyed acrobatics classes, had the best progress in the group and received praise from his teacher. Mark hated acrobatics classes and his movements were very awkward no matter how much effort he applied." Julia sighed and added: "One day Mark and Vlad came to me and said: 'Mom, we want to attend more classes we enjoy and stop attending classes we aren't good at.' And I did just what they asked. Every year I noticed how much progress my children made in their areas of interest and how correct this decision has been. Mark started writing his own songs, attended TV show castings and by the age of 20 is already a famous singer. Vlad on the other hand started winning sports competitions and by the age of 20 is performing in one of the most famous circuses in the world. Both my children are happy, successful and well-paid although their talents are completely different."

After my conversation with Julia and observing thousands of people in my life and how well or poorly their careers developed, I empirically have created a theory of 500 points. This theory says that how much success you achieve in your career is a multiplication of your talent and effort. For any type of work the talent scale is between 0 and 100 and the effort scale is between 0 and 5, hence the success in any area could be between 0 and 500. 0 means that you have no success at all and 500 means that you are one of the few most successful people in the world. The talent is fixed and is exactly how much gift nature has given you at birth and you can't make it higher or lower. If your talent is 0 – it means that you have no talent at all; if it's 100 this means that you are one of the best in the world. Effort on the other hand can be completely controlled by you. Effort is 0 if you don't do anything to apply your talent, and 5 if you are working with maximum productivity and efficiency to apply this talent. Many adults say to their children that if they work hard they can achieve anything in the world, however it is wrong and leads to many broken careers and lives.

Imagine that you want to be a rock star however your talent for singing is only 10 on a scale between 0 and 100. If you work as hard as you can and make your effort 5, your singing career success will be only 50 on a 0 to 500 scale and you will have no chances in competition with people who have 100 talent and only 2, 3 or 4 on the effort scale. Talent is significantly more important than effort in achieving big success or making a lot of money and it is fixed. Working hard is important, however even more important is identifying in what areas your talent is the highest on a scale from 0 to 100. Once you have identified your core talents it will be your lifelong goal to work hard and apply these core talents in a way that brings the most value to society.

Bill Gates became incredibly successful by applying his programming talent, Lady Gaga became incredibly successful by applying her singing talent and Michael Phelps became incredibly successful by applying his swimming talent. Now imagine that Bill Gates, Lady Gaga and Michael Phelps ignored their core talents and listened to their friends, relatives or classmates and chose a different promising career. For example Bill Gates pursued a swimming career, Lady Gaga pursued a programming career, and Michael Phelps pursued a singing career. Now you understand what a world with bad programmers, singers and swimmers will look like. Working hard to advance in your career and increase the amount of value that you generate for society is important, however even more important is identifying areas in which you have talent. How many people do you know that became successful without talent in their area and solely relying on their effort? I don't know anyone. When the most successful people in the world saw promising opportunities for which they didn't have talent, they ignored them because they knew that the only way to become successful is to spend most of your time applying your core talents. Your talents answer the question "Who am I?" and when you are true to yourself and stay "You" rather than try to be someone else, you become incredibly successful.

When I was a kid and attended karate classes my coach Alexander was once asked: "Who would win in a fight between a world champion in karate and a world champion in boxing?" He said: "Who would win in a fight between a bear and a shark? Of course a shark would win if the fight was in water and a bear if the fight was on the ground." From his answer I learned that each animal is strong in its natural medium and just as it's foolish for a fish to try climbing trees, for a bear to try to fly and for a dolphin to try to run, it's foolish for people trying to compete in areas for which they don't have a competitive advantage. The world pays the largest rewards for best results, you achieve best results when you have a competitive advantage over other people and the best competitive advantage is your talents. You can succeed and earn enough money in any career if you apply your talents and create a lot of value for society.

Everybody should be living in his or her natural medium in order to be successful: the shark should be swimming in the ocean, the bear should be walking on the ground, and you should spend most of your time working in areas where your talents are the strongest. If everybody in the world did things that they had the most talent for, it would be a perfect world in which all goods and services are of the highest quality and all people are happy and wealthy. Do what you are best at yourself, and delegate everything else to other people who are best in areas in which you are weak. Successful people build careers around their core talents, successful people build businesses around their core talents and when they see an interesting opportunity that doesn't utilize their core talents they skip it, because they know that long term they won't be able to create big value without using their competitive advantage. Using your strengths to help others will give your life the most meaning and your career the highest acceleration.

During our interview, a billionaire and one of the most successful entrepreneurs in Russia said: "I think that only 5% of people have talent for becoming an entrepreneur and building a big company." Looking back at my research of careers of thousands of people I realized that this is true not only for entrepreneurs but for all professions and empirically came to a 5% theory. This 5% theory says that for any profession that you can think of such as entrepreneur, teacher, soldier, lawyer, hairdresser, chef, programmer or singer, only 5% of the population has talent. The theory of 5% also says that talents in professions are evenly distributed and every single person has one or several distinct talents. Nature knows how many engineers, artists, coaches or scientists society needs and randomly distributes them among babies at birth. Your goal is to clearly identify in what areas you have talents and build your career around them. When you express your talents on a daily basis you get on a fast track to financial success and experience many more happy moments than an average person. Everybody has talents, figure out which ones you got through nature's lottery and then apply them your entire life.

You might think: "How can I identify what I am talented in?" Only you can give a clear answer, however to find it you may ask yourself the following questions: "If I could only do one thing all day long, what activity would contribute the greatest value to my company or organization?" "What can I do easily and well that is difficult for other people?" "What do I do that gets the most compliments and praise from other people?" After thinking about these questions, list all areas of work that you have ever tried in your life and rate your talent on a scale from 0 to 100, where 0 means lack of talent and 100 means one of the most talented people in the world. The areas in which you have the highest grades would be your talents, the areas in which your score is higher than 70 are certainly the candidates for your core talents list. If you have a talent for something, it shouldn't necessarily mean that you are the best in the world in this area, you should simply identify in which areas you are the strongest compared to other areas to decide where to invest most of your time and effort for highest results.

If you still don't know exactly what your talents are, give yourself time, think about your talents occasionally when you go for a walk or have a spare minute. In most cases what you have talent for coincides with what you are passionate about and figuring it out is one of the most important tasks in life. Once you have identified what area you are passionate about and have a talent for, think how to apply this skill in a way that brings maximum value for society. When passion, talent and value intersect – ability to earn money increases manifold and perhaps the most important step on the way to becoming financially successful is finding your own intersection. This intersection is your place in life where you will be the happiest and will earn the most.

Everyone is a genius. But if you judge a fish by its ability to climb a tree, it will live its whole life believing that it is stupid. – Albert Einstein

If you want to maximize your earning potential you need to make sure that you have talent for your work, you are passionate about your work and your work brings maximum value to society. You might think: "Hey, Andrii. That's just theoretical stuff. I have heard a lot about passion and talent from many people and that doesn't sound like a secret." Yes, actually the most effective things in the world aren't secrets, everybody has heard about them, however the difference between being insanely rich or broke is actually applying them. If you look back at your life you might see that your biggest fulfillment and success came from work that was located in this Millionaire's Triangle where you did what you had talent for, were passionate about and brought significant value to other people. Now imagine your future life, imagine how incredibly wealthy you will become and make a commitment to always do work that adheres to the Millionaire's Triangle principle. If from now on in the long-term perspective you commit only to work that is on the intersection of talent, passion and value for others, you will not only increase your earning potential manifold, but you will also be happier and find the perfect place in this life that was designed by Mother Nature particularly for YOU.

Set a long-term goal and move forward

Over 50 years ago sociologist Dr. Edward Banfield of Harvard University conducted a research trying to figure out a single predictor of why some people become financially successful and others don't. At the beginning of the research Banfield assumed that the answer would lie in such areas as education, social connections, family background, or intelligence, however the results surprised him. It turned out that the single most important factor in determining your success in life and work is a long-term vision and the further you look into the future when you do actions today, the more financially successful you become. For example people who are at the bottom of the social pyramid such as drug addicts or alcoholics do actions right now keeping in mind what they want to achieve in 2 hours, average people do actions right now keeping in mind where they want to be in 3 months, and the most successful people do actions right now keeping in mind where they want to be in 10 years. The further you look into the future while making decisions today, the more financially successful you will become, because your actions will be will be aligned in the same direction and will get you quickly to the destination that you have created in your imagination. If you want to be wealthy you need to have a long-term goal that motivates you to work daily and that gives your actions clear direction.

Average people move towards financial success on a blindfolded horse that moves chaotically and never gets anywhere. People with long-term goals move towards financial success on a horse with blinders that looks straight towards the goal, thinks about the goal, moves towards the goal and gets there through the shortest route. When you clearly know your most desired long-term goal you begin acting like a binary machine and making decisions becomes very easy. For every action that you intend to make, you ask yourself: "Does it bring me closer to my desired future?" If the answer is "yes" – you do it, and if the answer is "no" you don't. Remember that you are not who you are right now, but you are who you want to become. A person who won millions of dollars through a lottery but doesn't have a long-term goal is a poor student, and a poor student who doesn't have even money for food but works hard on his or her startup in a garage with a long-term goal to change the world for the better is a millionaire.

Ask yourself: "What did I want very much in my life but don't have it?" The answer is "Nothing." Because if you wanted something in the past as much as you want to breathe, you either already achieved it in the past, or are working hard right now for getting it in the near future. If you wanted something in the past and still don't have it, it means that most probably you didn't want it badly enough. Many people don't want their goals badly enough and when they realize how much effort it takes to achieve them, they stop halfway. If you want to become financially successful you not only should have a long-term goal, but you also need to make sure that this goal is so big, so exciting, so motivating that you don't care how much time, sweat or money it will require. Remember to choose your long-term goal carefully because you will not only spend a large part of your life achieving it but also this goal will define who you are. Ask yourself: "What do I want as much I want to breathe? What big goal do I want to achieve so much that even thinking about it makes me feel goose bumps? Why do I want to achieve it?" When you have a goal that is much bigger than primitive purchases and that is aimed for creating value for others, you will have as much energy and resources as needed for achieving it. The number one reason why people don't get what they want is that they don't know what they want. If you don't yet clearly know what big goal you want to achieve long term, think about it from time to time. Making a mental note to think about your big goal will help you find it sooner than you think. In most cases our big goal has always been under our nose but due to some unknown reasons we didn't clearly formulate it in the past.

One of the biggest drivers of financial success is a big long-term goal that is on the intersection of your passion and talents and is aimed to bring a lot of value to the world. Once you have clearly defined your long-term goal and have broken it into short-term sub-goals you will have shortened your way to financial success many times. Why? Because goals define our thoughts, thoughts define our actions and our actions define our results. Without a clear goal, thoughts in a head are chaotic and don't put in motion a financial success mechanism. When you have a long-term goal that you want to achieve as much as you want to breathe, all barriers for financial success such as laziness, fear, low self-esteem or lack of resources disappear. Once you define a long-term goal that you are passionate about, that utilizes your talents and that is aimed to bring a lot of value to others, your speed of becoming rich will increase manifold.

Some people die at 25 and aren't buried until 75. — Benjamin Franklin

When you are hunting elephants, don't get distracted chasing rabbits. — T. Boone Pickens

I can think of nothing less pleasurable than a life devoted to pleasure. — John D. Rockefeller

Money-making actions

Imagine that your long-term goal is one of the goods in a dreams store. If you want to achieve this goal you need to pay the price but instead of money, you pay with your actions. Financial success is achieved by reaching small, intermediate and big goals and you achieve them by taking effective actions. If you want to maximize the speed of movement towards financial success you need to first set a clear long-term goal and after that develop a habit of taking many effective actions every day. Your money machine produces money after processing raw materials that you supply to it, and these raw materials are your actions. There are 3 incredibly effective techniques for boosting productivity that have been tested on thousands of people around the world and proved their enormous effectiveness.

Visualization

A couple of years ago I listened to an interview given by an Olympic gold medalist in boxing, let's call him Jack. The interviewer asked, "Jack, could you ever have imagined that you would win a gold medal at the Olympic Games in Rio de Janeiro?" He said, "I have visualized this win since I was 9. Since I was 9 almost every day before I went to bed and right after I woke up I imagined the moment I am winning a gold medal in the Olympic Games and now it has finally happened."

A very important thing to understand about actions is that you don't take them out of the blue. Before taking any action in a direction towards a goal, you first think about a goal; thoughts always precede our actions. The first technique in this section is visualization and how it works can be very well summarized in the following phrase: "Where focus goes, energy flows and it eventually gets done."

Basically, if you think often about your favorite TV series, for example *Lost,* sooner or later you will watch the next episode, after you watch it you will have even more focus on watching *Lost* and you will be extremely likely to watch several episodes in a row until you realize that the day is already finished and you haven't accomplished anything important. Visualization works extremely well no matter if you use it to waste time or to make progress towards your goal. For example if you visualize fulfillment of your goal clearly in your mind several times throughout the day, you will not only make your mind think about ideas of how to accomplish it 24/7 but you will also accomplish significantly more actions in a direction of the goal. Remember that thoughts always precede actions, and if you want to force yourself to work productively you may accomplish this through a habit of thinking about your goal occasionally. The more you think about your goal, the more actions you will take eventually and the sooner it will get accomplished. Thinking about the successful accomplishment of the goal doesn't hurt, doesn't take much effort but is perhaps the most effective way to make yourself act, and successful people use visualization technique on a daily basis. Remember that the difference between a day when you accomplished many high-value tasks and a day when you accomplished no work at all may be the number of times that you focused your attention on your long-term goal. The human brain is organized in a way that if you see something clearly in your imagination your brain will try to do everything possible to make the picture in your head a reality.

My friend Jason asked me many years ago: "Andrii, do you know a visualization technique?" I said, "Yes, I do." Jason looked at me and continued: "Everybody knows but doesn't use it consciously. But I do use it daily, especially before going to bed and right after waking up. This makes my brain think subconsciously about my goal 24/7 and when I wake up I am focused already from the beginning of the day on actions that I need to do."

Kill the hope

One of the biggest blocks for actions is hope. Many people don't act because they hope that something positive will happen to them without their participation. Imagine that you have purchased stocks of a promising company and stopped working towards your financial success, hoping that in 10 years this stock will go up and you will become rich, however instead it went down. Imagine that you hope that your manager will raise your salary in a year and you don't take any action to work towards financial success, however at the end of the year due to some unexpected reason you didn't get a promotion. Imagine that you purchased a ticket in a national lottery and stopped working towards your financial success hoping that at the end of the month when the results are announced you will become a millionaire, however you lost. Very often people don't act simply because they are hoping that something positive will happen to them without their participation. It's not the problem that in this case you picked a wrong stock, you didn't get a promotion or bought a wrong ticket, the problem is that you actually lost ten years, one year or one month of time without taking actions towards financial success.

The technique "Kill the hope" works in the following way: In your imagination you kill the hope that something positive will happen to you without your participation. You take actions every day as usual towards financial success as if what you hope will happen won't actually happen. In this case, if a positive external thing actually does happen – perceive it as an unexpected gift. However if it doesn't happen, by that time you will have created great results and opened new opportunities for yourself by your actions. It doesn't mean that you need to be negative. Be positive and look optimistically into the future, believe that you will achieve your long-term goal, but kill the hope that blocks your actions, your results, and your success. It's your life and you can't assign responsibility for what happens to you to external circumstances that you don't control. You should take complete responsibility for your life and affect it through your actions.

Maximize the power of a present moment

In 1895, Italian economist Vilfredo Pareto discovered that 80% of the land in Europe is owned by 20% of the people and as a result the Pareto principle was born which states: for many events, roughly 80% of the effects come from 20% of the causes. Subsequent research found that 80% of revenue comes from 20% of customers, 80% of crimes are committed by 20% of criminals, 80% of illnesses are caused by 20% of diseases, 20% of the programming code has 80% percent of the errors, 20% of yard maintenance activities account for about 80% of how your yard actually looks and 20% of hazards cause 80% of injuries. The Pareto principle is extremely interesting because it applies to many areas of our life, however in this chapter it's particularly interesting how it relates to productivity. In productivity the Pareto principle says: 20% of the work you do accounts for 80% of results that you bring for your organization or company.

What if we eliminate 80% of actions and only do the 20% of actions with the highest results? The Pareto principle would still apply and 4% of actions (20% of 20% of original actions) would account for 64% of results (80% of 80% of original results). What if we eliminate actions with low results even further and begin doing only the 4% of original actions with highest results? The Pareto principle will apply again and 0.8% of original actions (20% of 20% of 20%) would account for 51.2% (80% of 80% of 80%) of original results. This means that if you do 5 different activities, 25 different activities or even 125 activities per day, just a single one of them would bring over 50% of results on your way to achieving the goal. No matter how many tasks you have for the day, just one of them will bring you over 50% of results and this task is called a golden task. You can work only on one task at a time and if you make sure that you always work on your current golden task you will be able to significantly increase your productivity and will move towards your successful financial future many times faster. When you work on a task that brings mediocre results, you aren't working on your golden task and are slowing a machine that produces effective actions necessary for purchase of a goal in a dreams store.

The third and final technique in this chapter is "Maximize the power of the present moment." When you work, keep in mind the following setting for your brain: "I need to maximize the power of the current moment. I will turn on my attention 100% and will work on a current task the best I can to get the maximum from the present moment. Life consists of short time frames and if I can get maximum results in a present moment, then I will get maximum from the next moment, then I will get maximum from the entire day and then my entire life will be extremely successful."

Consider time as your most precious currency that you need to invest with best returns. If you choose to always work on a task that brings the highest results at this point of your life and remind yourself from time to time to maximize the power of the present moment, you will be able to perform more high-value actions every day and it will give you an enormous acceleration to realizing your potential and building wealth.

Effective actions are money. If you want to have more money than now, you need to take more effective actions than now. Each action plants a seed on a success field. Some of them don't grow up, some of them grow up and give good results, and some of them give the biggest unexpected breakthroughs in your life. The biggest breakthroughs in life happen by accident, but we can increase probability of these accidents by our massive action in the right direction. The more effective actions you take, the more results you produce and results highly correlate with income. In order to increase the amount and quality of actions that you take use 3 techniques: visualize accomplishment of your goal, kill the hope that something positive out of your control will happen, and maximize the power of a present moment by giving

100% of yourself to the golden task that brings you highest results. If you are focused on a goal throughout the day, if you take complete responsibility for your future, and if you regularly encourage yourself to get maximum results out of the present moment, you will become incredibly successful. One of the distinct characteristics of people who created enormous wealth from scratch is that they take significantly more actions daily than an average person.

Most of us spend too much time on what is urgent and not enough time on what is important. – Stephen R. Covey

Earn more, earn more, earn more

Ask yourself: "In what profession can you become a millionaire?" If you look around, you may notice that huge amounts of money are earned by the BEST lawyers, doctors, singers, bankers, athletes, CEOs, entrepreneurs, celebrities. You might think: "If I want to become rich I should become one of them." And if you really try pursuing one of these professions without focusing on passion, talents and value, most probably you will have a miserable life doing what you don't enjoy every day and you will also earn very little money. Why? Because without passion, talents and focus on creation of value for others, you don't have any chance to become the BEST in any area.

The secret of becoming wealthy is not choosing a prestigious profession, but striving to become the BEST pursuing your vocation. If you enjoy being a nurse, you shouldn't strive to become a doctor or a lawyer, but you should maximize your earning potential as a nurse. For example, get additional certifications to become a nurse of a higher category and move to a prestigious hospital with higher salaries. If you want to become rich, don't strive to become a millionaire no matter through which profession, but choose the profession for which you have a calling and later strive to increase your income in this profession. If your vocation is being a nurse, you will never earn as much as the best doctors, but you can earn more than other nurses and become the best nurse. If you are in your place and are one of the best in your profession, you will get recognition from colleagues and clients, you will enjoy every day of your work, and you will have a decent lifestyle.

One of my friends, Mark, chose the profession of a school math teacher and enjoys his work very much. As you know, teachers don't earn a lot of money, however Mark is earning several times more than an average teacher. He shared with me what allowed him to increase his income while pursuing his vocation: "Andrii, I just did my job really well and became one of the best teachers in my first school and got a recognition as a teacher of the year. After that I moved to a prestigious private school and my salary got higher, in a few years I began preparing students for international math Olympiads and for university applications. In addition to a private school salary I am also earning additional income through preparing a national team for math competitions, through private tutoring, through being a YouTube video blogger talking about math, and through writing math textbooks. As a result although I am still a math teacher I am able to earn several times more than my colleagues, I love what I do, and I have enough money to afford whatever I want."

Remember that you should strive to be a natural millionaire, you need to first find your vocation, and later aim to maximize your earning potential in this job. The life of people who are ready to take any job just to make money is usually miserable. They think they will be able t odo what they enjoy once they are rich, but they never achieve their goals. If you don't have a passion or talent for being a lawyer, a doctor or an entrepreneur please don't be a lawyer, a doctor or an entrepreneur. Choose a job according to your passion and talents and after that maximize value that you create for other people and simultaneously your primary source of income will increase. I call people who try to become the best at their jobs even if they are not well-paid – the natural millionaires. Not everyone will become a billionaire but everyone should strive to become a natural millionaire, everyone can earn more doing his or her favorite job.

Earn more as an employee

Remember the weekend when I met Jason, a serial entrepreneur and a billionaire, and his friend Adam who built an astonishing career on Wall Street and ended up working as a chef in a small restaurant pursuing his vocation? After a walk during which Jason shared with me the concept of The Wealth Formula we returned to his house. Adam, Jason and I sat on armchairs around the fireplace in the living room and enjoyed a hot chocolate that Jane made for us.

Adam said: "Before, I thought that in order to be happy and rich you should be a doctor, a lawyer, an entrepreneur, an investment banker or a rock star, now I understand that in order to be happy and rich you should aim to bring as much value to society as you can by working in a job for which you have talent and passion."

Jason sipped his hot chocolate and said: "I agree with you, the first and most important step in The Wealth Formula is to increase your primary source of income, and working on something that you are passionate about and have talents for and that brings value to others is the only right approach. Adam, tell Andrii your techniques to maximize earning potential if you are an employee, and later I will share with him how to maximize earning potential if you are an entrepreneur."

I said: "I feel that something is already shifting in my head. Adam, so how do you maximize your earnings as an employee?"

Adam continued: "I have observed numerous people who have built incredible careers within a short period of time and realized that there are two principles that all of them followed. Anyone who takes these principles to heart and follows them, I have no doubt, will earn as an employee more and more and more.

"The first technique says: To earn more you need to aim to earn more. Although this technique sounds simple, very few people actually aim to earn more. If you want to earn more you simply need to take actions that will affect your future income. You may obtain an additional certification that will impact your income, you may strive to get more responsibility in your role that will impact your income, you may change an organization that you work for or you may work hard to get a performance bonus. Although it seems obvious that if you want to earn more you need to make attempts to earn more and take actions that may impact your income, the majority of people don't use this technique.

"The second technique says: Work for a company like you are an owner. If you are an employee and want to increase income you need to perceive the company that you work for as your own, take initiative and bring it as much value as you can. If you work having in mind that 'It's my own company,' you will enjoy your work more, you will give it everything you can and it will be obvious for others. People who work for a company like they own it are the first to get a promotion or a pay raise."

The techniques I earned from Adam are incredibly effective and if you are an employee just following them will significantly improve your income. Not everyone should strive to become an entrepreneur, the majority of people are happy being an employee their entire life. If you choose the life of an employee, strive to be the best in your job and bring as much value as you can to your organization. You will not only increase your primary source of income significantly but will also be able to spend many hours, days and months doing a job that you love.

It doesn't matter if you are a filing clerk, an athlete, an accountant or a bartender. All that matters is that you do whatever you can to be the best. – Mark Cuban

Earn more if you are an entrepreneur

When Adam finished sharing the techniques for earning more as an employee Jason took over and said: "As an employee the amount of value that you can create for people is limited, because no matter how talented or productive you are, there are a limited amount of hours that you can work per day. If you want to increase the amount of value that you create for others and as a result your income even further, you need to become an entrepreneur. As an entrepreneur you will have to create a mechanism that takes the work of other people and resources on input and produces value for customers on output. How much value you can create for society using entrepreneurship isn't limited and as a result your earning potential isn't limited as well.

"Andrii, entrepreneurship isn't a separate career path – it's simply a multiplier of your efforts and a multiplier of YOU. To explain how this multiplier works, let me briefly share the career path of my friend Jim, who owns the restaurant in which Adam works as a chef.

"Jim has a talent and passion for cooking. He began his career as chef's assistant in a small restaurant, after several promotions he became a chef in a big prestigious restaurant in New York. Jim realized that although thousands of people enjoyed his meals, he couldn't increase the amount of value that he brought to the world by staying a chef. Your earning potential is limited if you are selling time for money no matter how much it costs. If you want to be rich sell not your time, but solve a problem and get paid for results.

"With a partner, Jim opened first a small restaurant which soon became successful. A few years later Jim is managing already a chain of 15 restaurants and the amount of value that he brings to the world through the entrepreneurship multiplier increased dozens of times as did his income. Entrepreneurship significantly increased the amount of people who Jim's talent and passion for cooking touches. If you feel that you have a talent and passion for creating your own company and are ready to go through all the intermediate difficulties and failures associated with it, go ahead and do so, as entrepreneurship is a multiplier that can increase positive impact from your effort numerous times. Entrepreneurship multiplier is a tool that the majority of the richest people in the world actively use. The sense of entrepreneurship is to bring value to other people on a mass scale and the more value you bring, the more gratitude in the form of money you will receive.

"Andrii, remember The Wealth Formula that I talked about during our walk along the ocean beach? (Income – Cost of Living)*(Interest on Investment) = Growing Wealth. Entrepreneurship is not only the multiplier for your primary income, but it is also the best investment option for your savings. After you have saved money you need to invest it with the highest return on investment and the lowest risk so that your money works for you and brings you even more money."

I looked at Jason and asked, "There are so many different investment options. Why is entrepreneurship the best one?"

Jason smiled and said: "It's a good question. The best investment option is the one that gives the highest return on investment with the lowest risk. The best investment opportunity is putting money in a business that you have talents for, you are passionate about and that is aimed to improve lives of other people. Why? Because you have talent for your work, you understand it, you control it, you are an expert in it, you have years of experience in it, you are passionate about it and this gives a significant competitive advantage which reduces risk and increases potential return.

"Let's talk about the numbers. If you just have started a small company and it took off during the first several years, your return on investment could be 100% per year or above. If your company is already of average size and it's doing well, your return on investment could be 20% or above. If your company is one of the biggest in the country and is doing well, your return on investment could be 10% or above. All other investment options that exist give less than 10% per year with a comparable level of risk. If you are an entrepreneur or an employee, invest as much money as you can that may increase your primary source of income and only after that move to the second-best investment option. Investing in your primary source of income, whether it is a company or a career, is the investment option with the highest return and the lowest risk. Completely passive investments don't give such a great return so to get rich fast you must make your own business or grow on the career ladder."

Don't start a company unless it's an obsession and something you love. If you have an exit strategy, it's not an obsession. — Mark Cuban

Income ladder

What if in order to become rich you didn't have to work on bringing value for other people but could simply win millions of dollars in a lottery and live happily ever after?

In 1961 a British cake-factory worker Vivian Nicholson won $5 million in the Littlewood Football Pool lottery. A reporter asked: "What do you plan to do with your winnings?" She answered: "Spend, spend, spend!" And Vivian did just that, she purchased expensive and lavish sports cars, fur coats, jewelry, exotic vacations and over the next few years depleted her fortune completely. During this spending marathon Vivian managed to become a widow three times and an alcoholic. She tried suicide twice, spent time in a mental institution and lived the last years of her life on a modest government pension, without a family, without work, and without savings.

Billy Bob Harrell Jr., after being laid off from several jobs, became an employee stocking electrical-supply shelves of a Home Depot store. He was having a hard time providing for himself, his wife and their three children. Every week he purchased lottery tickets in hopes of solving his financial problems and in June 1997 he got lucky and won $37 million in a Texas lottery. Once he received this money he went on vacation with his family to Hawaii, purchased expensive houses, cars and paintings. He also made large contributions to his church, helped the poor, and gave cash presents to friends. Less than two years after winning the lottery Billy Bob Harrell Jr. was broke, divorced and depressed. On May 22, 1999, Billy Bob stripped himself naked and shot himself in the chest with a shotgun. Shortly before his suicide he told his financial adviser: "Winning the lottery is the worst thing that ever happened to me."

In 2002, a 19-year-old garbage collector named Michael Carroll won $15 million in the British National Lottery. He began making expensive presents to his family members and friends. In a year he was already spending over $2,000 every day on crack cocaine and hosting drug and alcohol-fueled parties at his recently purchased expensive house. After his wife requested a divorce, Michael added sex to his other addiction. Over the next few years he spent over $200,000 on prostitutes. In 2010 when Michael went broke he ended up working again as a garbage collector. He said that now his life is much easier than when he was a millionaire.

So why don't the majority of lottery winners manage to increase the amount of money that has fallen on them and why do they sometimes feel miserable? The answer to this is that they simply aren't ready for managing such big sums of money, they artificially jumped over many rungs on the income ladder and weren't ready for the pressure. People who manage one million dollars are solving problems for ten million dollars, and if you jumped from earning a minimum wage to being a millionaire without going through intermediate points, the scale of problems that you will face may break you. A billionaire who went bankrupt can start again and earn a billion dollars from scratch because he or she is prepared for solving problems for ten billion dollars. A poor person who won a lottery may be scared by the scale of problems associated with it, and after getting rid of all the money will return to the level of problems he or she is comfortable with. According to the *New York Daily News* 70% of lottery winners end up broke within seven years.

Let's review how rich people climb the income ladder with the example of Richard Branson. At the age of 14 in 1968, after a failed business of growing and selling Christmas trees, Branson founded a student magazine which in a year made his net worth $65,000. During the next ten years Richard Branson sold records by mail order, opened his record shop, created the Virgin Records label and his net worth was estimated at $6.5 million by 1979. During the next twenty years Branson founded new companies including Virgin Airways, Virgin Trains, Virgin Cosmetics, Virgin Mobile, Virgin Games and by 1997 his net worth was already estimated as $2.1 billion. As you can see, in order to get from nothing to becoming insanely rich, you need to go through intermediate points on the income ladder. When you move from goal to goal and get used to problems of the current scale, you can increase your income and the scale of problems that you work on.

If instead of dreaming about winning a lottery, you set a goal to double your income, and after you reach this goal to double it again, and after you reach this goal to double it again, you will be able to smoothly increase your income to any point. The ladder approach will allow you not only to earn more money, but also to not lose it and to adjust yourself to the level of problems that are associated with each subsequent level of income.

If you try to teach an elementary school math student how to solve high school problems, the child may lose faith in his or her abilities and fail. However, if you teach a child how to solve elementary school problems, after that how to solve middle school problems, after that the child would be comfortable working on high school problems. If you want to become insanely rich you need to first go through elementary school money problems, after that through middle school money problems and then you will be ready for high school money problems. If you asked rich people at the beginning of the path: "How to become a billionaire?" they would answer: "I have no idea." But after reaching each intermediate point on the income ladder they see how to make a next step and then a next step and then a next step and once many steps are added they end up being incredibly wealthy. Set intermediate financial goals and by moving between them you will accumulate wealth with a higher probability than if you attempt to do a single long-distance jump towards your ultimate destination.

Theory of social tribes

Whatever you do, you are a member of a social tribe that has losers who have a small income, the majority who have average income and stars who have awesome income. In each social tribe the losers and the majority envy the stars and hope to become stars one day themselves. Teachers, police officers, entrepreneurs, dancers, soldiers, taxi drivers, nurses, doctors, hairdressers, other mini societies all have their own social tribes and benchmarks of what is bad, average and awesome. For example, for the USA in the hairdressers tribe the low income is $15,000 per year, the average is $20,000 and awesome is $40,000. In the software developers tribe the low income is $60,000 per year, average is $100,000 and awesome is $300,000. In the billionaires tribe a low income is $10 million per year, average is $100 million per year and awesome is $1 billion per year. When you are a novice in a social tribe, members of the tribe teach you how to live and progress within the boundaries of this mini society. You need to understand that you grow the most not when you progress between statuses in a current social tribe, but when you move to a social tribe that is one or several levels above and try to climb the income ladder in a more advanced social tribe. It's better to be a loser among software developers than a star among hairdressers and it's better to be a loser among billionaires than a star among software developers.

Several years ago I shared a theory of social tribes with my friend Andzej when we met for a cup of coffee and he told me how he intuitively used this theory when he studied at school: "Andrii, I studied in an ordinary middle school where fighting and communication skills were valued more than academic performance among students. I wasn't interested in math and if I rated myself in my school I would be somewhere among the losers. In the social tribe that the school represented, a star was Max as he easily grasped all the concepts, received only A grades and got constantly praised by our math teacher.

"After middle school after intense preparation by some miracle I got accepted to a technical high school that was situated right across the street from my middle school. This high school had a much stronger focus on math than my previous school, it had much stronger students and here instead of fighting or communication skills, academic performance was the highest value. If I rated myself among students I would certainly be among the losers. After couple of months I got really interested in math because it was taught in a much more engaging way than at my first school and started devoting most of my spare time to solving difficult problems. Within two years from a loser I became average, after that I became a star, and then the strongest among the stars. I easily grasped all concepts, received only A grades and constantly was praised by our math teacher.

"One year before graduation I moved to my third school, which not only was strong in math, but was one of the most advanced schools in the country and had many winners of international math competitions. When I came to the first class I realized that I was not a star anymore, but a member of the majority at best. For months I worked harder than ever before on developing my problem solving skills, I interacted with the stars on a daily basis, and aimed for a benchmark that was incredibly high. By the end of the year I didn't manage to become the best in my school, however I became the weakest among the stars.

"The last math competition before graduation was organized by the strongest technical university in the country. The winners would receive a full scholarship to study in this university. When the competition ended I noticed Max from my first school near the exit of the building. After some small talk I asked: "How many problems did you solve?" He said: "Nah, I didn't solve any, they were incredibly difficult." He asked me: "How many did you solve?" And I answered: "I solved them all, they were relatively easy." At this point I realized that changing schools, changing benchmarks of what is weak, average and strong, changing social tribes had been the reason I became so strong in math. Had I studied math hard in my first school I would have become average, or like Max at best."

When you are in a social tribe, people in this tribe will affect what you think, will impact your aspirations, will share ideas, and will have the same values as you. The people that you interact with can help you incredibly to progress within the tribe's boundaries, what they can't help with is progress beyond the tribe's boundaries. When you are average in your social tribe, the biggest breakthroughs in life happen when you change your social tribe. When you are a star in your current social tribe, although you may feel comfortable, it's awful in terms of increasing income because you stop improving. On the other hand, if you move to a more advanced social tribe with the status of a loser and are passionate about moving up to the majority or the stars, you will become successful as never before. Consciousness is contagious and constant exposure to people who are more successful may expand your thinking and skyrocket your income. People around you set a bar that you try to reach, they help to clarify the path towards this bar, and they share energy necessary for reaching goals that are normal for this particular social tribe. When your standard of what is normal is raised, your motivation for working harder and smarter for creating value for society increases. Put yourself in a medium where your type of work is appreciated and done on a very high level. When your internal strength is combined with external strength of a social tribe, the speed of climbing up an income ladder increases.

You might think: "So how do I change my social tribe?" There are numerous ways to make this change, however often it is associated with changing a city, changing a company, changing a career path, starting a business, getting additional education, expanding a social circle, or just dreaming bigger.

Millionaire's mindset

Millionaire's glasses

Once upon a time in the same city there lived a poor Joe and a wealthy Sam. Joe and Sam had the same height, same weight, same talents, same education, same connections however after graduation Joe began working at minimum wage and retired working at minimum wage. Sam however took initiative in his work and grew on a career ladder. At some point he started a business, went bankrupt, started another business, went bankrupt again, started his third business which eventually succeeded and by the time of retirement he was a multimillionaire. If you think why two seemingly similar people had very different financial futures the obvious answer would be – because they took different actions throughout their lives. The really interesting question is: "Why did they take different actions throughout their lives?"

No matter how much information you know, you act daily according to a very small amount of beliefs that are set in stone in your head. If you ask a billionaire how to become rich he or she might answer: "Set ambitious goals, and take massive action to achieve them." You might think: "Hey, this billionaire just wants to get rid of me. The billionaire knows the real secret, but doesn't want to reveal it and gave me a generic answer that I heard many times before." Often rich and poor know the same information, but they have different beliefs set in stone in their heads. In this case for poor people a tip, "Set ambitious goals, and take massive action" might be generic useless information, but for rich people it's a belief set in stone in their heads that they cherish, to which they attribute all their success and according to which they act daily.

Every time Joe woke up he saw the world through the lens of the beliefs set in stone in his head: "Money is earned by hard and unpleasant work." "All rich are bad people and earned their wealth in dishonest ways." "I can't become rich because I wasn't born in a wealthy family." When Joe went out of the house he saw confirmation that his beliefs were true everywhere, because he was looking for confirmations and filtered everything else. These beliefs impacted all actions that Joe took and according to them he earned little money with hard, unpleasant work and didn't make any attempts to increase his income. Sam on the other hand woke up and saw the world through the lens of other beliefs set in stone in his head: "By earning more money, I am creating good for the world." "There are plenty of opportunities to earn more." "I should always do work that I am passionate about and have a talent for." "I will always succeed if I make enough attempts." When Sam went out of the house he saw confirmation that his beliefs were true everywhere, because he was looking for confirmations and filtered everything else.

Those few beliefs that are set in stone in your head define a lens through which you look at the world and this lens affects your thoughts, actions and eventually financial future. If you want to become rich you need to make sure that your core beliefs help you to accumulate wealth rather than set obstacles on your way. Beliefs affect thoughts, thoughts affect actions and actions affect results. If one day you get tired and say: "Nah, it's too difficult. I am not good enough to become wealthy," say "Hi" to your internal Joe. However remember that nearby lives Sam who had the same education as you, same talents as you, same connections as you and became rich because the beliefs set in stone in his head were different.

Rich brain, poor brain

There are two types of brain that people are using: a poor brain and a rich brain. A poor brain is responsible for finding excuses: "For getting rich you need connections and I don't have any." "I am not getting a promotion because my manager doesn't appreciate my work." "I can't start a business because I am the breadwinner in my family and can't risk it." A poor brain finds excuses for any problem and literally says: "I found a very reasonable excuse. Nothing depends on my actions and my life is in the hands of circumstances. If nothing depends on my actions I simply don't have to do anything and doing nothing is comfortable."

A rich brain is responsible for finding solutions and creates questions in the subconscious: "What business should I start?" "How can I increase my income even further?" "How can I sell more goods and services?" "How can I increase my salary?" The rich brain finds solutions for any problem and literally says: "Everything depends on my actions. I can find solutions for any problem. I need to take action right now."

A poor brain finds answers for the question: "Why I can't?" and a rich brain finds answers for the question "How can I?" Henry Ford once said: "Whether you think you can, or you think you can't – you're right."

All people have both rich and poor brains, however poor people rely more on the poor brain and rich people rely more on the rich brain. Whenever you face an obstacle that seems insurmountable it's OK to get sad for a little while, however don't forget to turn on your rich brain and find a solution that will help you to take the next step towards financial success. Use your rich brain as often as possible because it always finds numerous solutions for any problem, the only time it doesn't find solutions is when your poor brain already has found an excuse.

Rich people focus on opportunities, poor people focus on obstacles. – Harv Ecker

Happiness first, wealth later

In 2006 the Pew Research Center conducted a survey among 18-25-year-olds, which revealed that for 81% of young people at the beginning of their career getting rich is either their number one or number two goal. The majority of people who want to become rich think: "First I need to reach my money goal and only after that I will be happy. I will exercise, I will eat healthy food, I will take vacations and I will do work that I am passionate about." In fact a goal to become rich is often an excuse for being unhappy: "I will suffer for several years but once I am rich I will begin living happily." Interestingly in reality this works vice versa – you first become happy (exercise, eat healthy food, take vacations, do work that you are passionate about) and only after that you become rich.

In a meta-analysis of 225 academic studies, researchers Sonja Lyubomirsky, Laura King and Ed Diener found that happy employees have on average 31% higher productivity, their sales are 37% higher and their creativity is three times higher. If you interact with people who are already rich you might realize that happiness is a reason for wealth and not a consequence. If you can't be happy with money that you currently have, chances are that you won't be happy with any amount of money, and since happiness is an important factor on the way towards financial success, chances are that you will never reach it.

Imagine that you have $1 billion and think how you would live with more money than you could ever spend. What things would you do that would make you happy? Now begin doing all these things with money and resources that you already have. This approach will bring you to wealth much faster than if you postpone happiness until better days. In order to attract money you need to be in a good mood most of the time and be happy even without a lot of money. Remember that happiness doesn't come after success, but happiness attracts success in the first place.

One of the most powerful tools in millionaires' arsenal is their mindset. When your core beliefs are helping you to climb the income ladder, when you utilize your rich brain to find solutions for problems and when you are happy at the beginning of your path towards financial success, you begin attracting money faster than the majority of people can only dream about.

What do you need more money for?

One day a rich businessman came for vacation to a heavily secluded island and noticed a poor native lying in a hammock all day long doing nothing. He approached and said: "I see that you are poor, why don't you collect bananas from palm trees and sell them to tourists?" The native looked at the businessman and asked: "What for?" The businessman continued: "With this money you will be able to start a company and hire other natives to collect even more bananas and you will earn even more money." The native asked again: "What for?" The businessman said: "After that you will be able to buy a boat, go fishing and sell fish to tourists. Then buy more boats and hire more natives to earn even more money." The native asked: "What for?" The businessman said: "With this money you will be able to sell more and more products, then build a multinational corporation and then become insanely rich." The native asked: "What for?" The businessman said: "Once you have so much money you won't have to work anymore, you will be able to come to a heavenly island and lie in a hammock all day long doing nothing." The native smiled and said: "I already have this."

My friend Jason, the serial entrepreneur and billionaire, said: "If you want to earn one billion dollars, one day you will have to risk one hundred million. The biggest reason why people don't become rich is because they are comfortable with what they already have. The biggest enemy of wealth is the word 'enough'."

Imagine John who is primarily motivated by money. John will increase his income more and more until he reaches his level of comfort. At this level John will stop trying to increase his income because subconsciously he understands that to earn significantly more he needs to risk what is already comfortable and experience discomfort at least temporarily. John will think: "I already have enough. Now my goal is to protect my comfort and make sure this income level stays the same forever." If your primary motivation is comfort, then after you reach a certain level of wealth you will stop climbing the income ladder because you fear losing what you already have. The majority of people are comfortable with their current income and if you want to become rich you need to give your internal native lying in a hammock a very clear answer to the question: "What do I need significantly more money for?"

Many people think: "I first need to become rich, and after that I will think what to do with the money." Actually it doesn't work this way. At first you need to clearly identify what you need money for, and after that money will be attracted. If you consciously think: "Well, I definitely want to become rich," then your internal native will say: "It's so comfortable to live with your current income level. Do you know that striving to earn more money may be associated with stress, difficulties and a lot of work? So if you want me to stand up from a hammock and do something, please give me a really strong reason that you need more money for." There are three major reasons that can motivate you to increase wealth.

Money for comfort and pleasure

The first motivation to earn more money is increasing comfort of life. Create a list of 100 wishes that could improve your quality of life and write next to each of them a cost. These could be either material possessions such as a house or a car, or experiences like a vacation or education. It's important to stretch you mind and go beyond obvious things and write the list of 100 items that include all desires that you want to fulfill if money wasn't an issue. Now add the cost of all items in the list and write down an approximate overall sum. You need to see this sum and mentally get used to it to increase your money capacity. To have more money, you need to have desires on which to spend it, without desires money doesn't come.

Everybody has a level of income that is associated with comfort. In 2010 Princeton University researchers Elizabeth Dunn and Michael Norton examined poll data from nearly 500,000 U.S. households and figured out that money improves happiness until an income level of $75,000 per year and after this amount income doesn't affect happiness anymore. No matter how high your level of comfortable income is, and as you see from the Princeton research usually this level is relatively low, after you reach it you might stop attempting to earn significantly more because of fear to risk what you already have. If you want to be rich rather than to just have a comfortable life, you need a stronger motivation for money than just physical possessions or experiences. Remember that one day to earn $1B you will have to risk $100M, one day to earn $100M you will have to risk $10M, one day to earn $10M you will have to risk $1M and a person who is motivated primarily by comfort would never take this risk.

Everybody has a "money scenario" of how much money he or she should earn and in which way. For example if a homeless man needs money he would ask for change on a street corner, the idea of finding a job would never strike his head because being poor is comfortable. If a hairdresser needs money she would find a job in a beauty salon, the idea of starting a business would never strike her head, because a moderate income is comfortable. If a billionaire needs money he would create a multinational corporation, the idea of begging for change or finding a job would never strike his mind because being poor is uncomfortable, having a moderate income is uncomfortable but being a billionaire is comfortable. As you can see, you can be comfortable at any income level and in order to get out of this comfort zone, to change your behavior pattern, to make a step towards an unknown you might need a significantly stronger reason than purchasing expensive goods or experiences.

Money for financial freedom and independence

In a fictional land near the sea there lived a poor old fisherman and his wife. One day the man came to the beach, threw a fishing rod into the sea and caught a golden fish. The golden fish said: "Old man, please return me to the sea and for this I will fulfill three wishes for you." The man thought for a second and said: "I want to live in a beautiful and expensive house." The fish said: "Let be it." And a beautiful, expensive house appeared in place of the old man's poor hut. The man said: "Wow! The house looks awesome. My second wish is to have a luxury car." The fish said: "Let be it." And a beautiful new luxury car appeared next to the old man's house. The old man rubbed his head and thought much longer this time, he thought and thought and thought and finally said: "My third wish is to have an unlimited amount of wishes."

In 2000 researchers in the National Opinion Research Center conducted a survey among adult Americans asking how free they feel. 70% of respondents said that they were "completely free" or "very free" and 25% said that they were "moderately free." The survey also revealed that people who felt "completely free" or "very free" were twice as likely to say that they are very happy about their lives than those who were "moderately free." Freedom and happiness are highly correlated and one way to become happier is adding financial freedom to all the other freedoms that you have. Financial freedom is a passive income that generates you so much money each month that you can live a comfortable life even without working. When you can work not for survival but for higher causes, your happiness and life satisfaction increase. When you are financially free you can live like if you have caught a golden fish and it fulfilled your wish to have an unlimited amount of wishes.

The intermediate point towards financial freedom is financial independence which means that your basic survival needs are met even without your work. Financial independence equals 150*(Minimum expenditures per month) and once you invest this sum at 8% yearly interest you will obtain the necessary amount of money for your minimum monthly expenditures passively from interest even without your work. Minimum expenditures per month is the lowest amount of money that you need to survive, the more modest your life potentially can be the lower is the sum of money necessary for financial independence. Calculate what your personal financial independence number is and get used to it. If you accumulate this number, you will become financially independent and no matter what happens in your career you will definitely survive thanks to your financial independence cushion. Knowing that you have such a cushion will make you feel good and allow you to take risks necessary to climb the income ladder more easily.

Financial freedom means that you can have the life you want even without working, relying solely on passive income from investments. Financial freedom equals 150*(Desired income per month), where desired income is how much would you love to spend per month without limiting yourself in anything. If you invest this amount of money at 8% interest per year you will be able to receive your desired income passively every month from the interest. Calculate how much financial freedom is for you and get used to this number. If you accumulate this number you will know that no matter what happens in your career, your life will be comfortable anyway. Knowing that you have such a cushion will allow you to work not for comfort but for a higher purpose and will make you happier because financial freedom will be added to all the other freedoms that you have. Once the fear of losing comfort is replaced by love for the work you do and motivation of fulfilling your life mission, the speed of moving towards financial success increases manifold.

Money for a life mission

If your only motivation for work is earning money for a comfortable life then at some point you will have enough and will stop setting ambitious goals because of fear of risking what you already have. If you want to become rich you need a significantly stronger motivation for work than comfort, and this motivation is – to significantly improve lives of people around the world. This motivation should have such a significant emotional response in your heart that you could call it your life mission.

Life is fair and really big money is attracted not for petty needs like buying a car, a house, or clothing but for a big specific goal targeted to bring value for society. Rich people know that in order to attract enormous wealth they need to focus on bringing enormous value for other people, and when they create this enormous value they will have their share of money attracted from thankful clients. If you focus on changing many lives for the better, your work will be appreciated and as a side benefit you will get enough money to maintain any level of comfort. However if you focus primarily on earning more money just to improve your own life, the world will sense it, and will hesitate sending wealth your way.

Nature somehow has programmed in people an internal need to improve the lives of others and move humanity forward. If you do what you are passionate about, if you utilize your talents, aim to create value for others and pursue your life mission, money will come your way in abundance, part of which you can spend on your own comfort. However if you ignore what nature wants from you and are focused only on getting money for yourself, no matter in which way, then becoming wealthy will be significantly more difficult and in the long term money won't bring satisfaction. After communicating with hundreds of self-made millionaires I came to the conclusion that all of them are motivated by the most powerful motivation in the world – fulfilling their life mission. No matter what your current income, no matter what income you dream to have, make sure that your attention is focused not on money, but on a big goal from which many other people would benefit because it's the only way to become rich both financially and spiritually. Life mission is like a money magnet – the bigger and more significant your mission is, the more easily necessary resources will be attracted for it. Motivation of life mission is many, many, many times more powerful than motivation of pursuing comfort or financial freedom. Money isn't a goal, but a resource for achieving goals. The bigger your goal, the more value it brings for society, the more money it attracts. If you refocus your attention from becoming rich to fulfilling your life purpose you will activate an internal mechanism for attracting wealth that somehow is programmed in all people by nature.

The biggest reasons why people don't get rich is because they are comfortable with what they have, they fear losing what they already have and they don't know exactly what they need more money for. Three reasons why you may want to work hard, overcome obstacles, and suffer through failures on the way to financial success are a desire to increase comfort of life, a desire to obtain financial freedom, and a desire to fulfill your big mission that will improve the lives of other people. The motivation to fulfill your big mission is many times more powerful than the other two motivations, it doesn't set a limit of how much money you can attract, and it is a must-have if you want to not just slightly increase your income but to make it dozens, hundreds or thousands of times higher. Remember that the world is fair and supplies large sums of money only for big goals that could improve not only your life but also the lives of many other people. Such goals are a vacuum cleaner for money, and you are a pipe through which money comes for creating value for society.

I think everybody should get rich and famous and do everything they ever dreamed of so they can see that it's not the answer. – Jim Carrey

Money was never a big motivation for me, except as a way to keep score. The real excitement is playing the game. – Donald Trump

Save like a millionaire

Spend less than you earn

The Wealth Formula says: (Income – Cost of Living)*(Interest on Investment) = Growing Wealth. Basically to become rich you need to spend less than you earn and profitably invest the difference so that your money creates even more money for you. In order to increase your net worth, having a high income is important however at least as important is to reduce your cost of living to maximize the amount of money you have available for investing.

In the 1960s and early 1970s Stanford University professor Walter Mischel conducted a famous marshmallow experiment. Children were left in a room for 15 minutes alone with one marshmallow and had a choice to either eat this marshmallow immediately or to get two marshmallows at the end of this time period. When these children grew up, their results on the marshmallow test were compared with their performance in life, and it was obvious that people who could sacrifice short-term gratification for long-term larger gratification were significantly more successful by all measures than people who decided to eat a single marshmallow right away when they were children.

The majority of adults have a child's mentality that would rather have one marshmallow right now than two marshmallows later. Basically, a worker spends everything he or she has earned by the end of the year. A manager has a slightly better house, slightly better car, slightly better clothes than a worker but still spends everything he or she has earned by the end of the year. A director has a slightly better house, slightly better car, slightly better clothes than a manager but still spends everything he or she has earned by the end of the year. For becoming rich it is important not how much you earn per year, but how much you are able to save per year. If you earn a million dollars and spend a million dollars by the end of the year, your net worth equals the net worth of a homeless person and is zero. When you begin your journey towards financial success you need to learn how to manage money that you already have according to the Wealth Formula: spend less than you earn and invest what is saved by the end of the year so that money begins working for you.

In The Millionaire Factory system I define that you are rich if you spend on life less than 25% of your yearly income, so that you have 75% of income left for investments that will bring interest to you. If you are rich, within this 25% of income you can afford yourself any lifestyle you want, you have achieved significant success and you have a right to enjoy this part of income as you want: cars, yachts, jets, houses, clothing, restaurants – whatever you please. If you are not yet rich according to The Millionaire Factory system definition you need to limit your cost of living to maximize the difference between income and spending and this will skyrocket your speed of moving towards financial success.

Let's return to my weekend with Jason and Adam. When we were sitting in the living room enjoying a fire in the fireplace at some point I asked, "Jason, I know many people who are reluctant to take risks in their careers saying that they are afraid to fail and not be able to pay their bills. What would you recommend to them?" Jason breathed deeply and said:

"When I studied in college our professor said: 'You have 4 years to start a business, if you don't start a business within 4 years of college you will never do so.' I would say that the professor was only partially right: You have indefinite time to start a business or to make a career change if you are willing to continue living like a student. If you have a high cost of living that consumes your entire income – you voluntarily wear handcuffs that limit opportunities and kill prospects for future financial success. If you live frugally, you increase your opportunities, reduce stress over bills, and are able to take any necessary risks in your career or business to get to financial success through the fastest route." After a short discussion Jason and Adam agreed that before you become rich according to The Millionaire Factory definition your goal is to do everything to increase the difference between your income and spending by reducing cost of living. After you become rich you can buy whatever you want to make your life comfortable as long as it is within 25% of your income.

By the way Warren Buffett, founder of Berkshire Hathaway, whose net worth is around $60 billion, lives in a 5-bedroom house in Omaha that he purchased in 1958 for $31,500. Although he could purchase any car in the world he drives himself in a Cadillac XTS which costs around $45,295. Ingvar Kamprad, founder of IKEA, whose net worth was estimated to be $39.3 billion, flies economy class, drives a decades-old Volvo and frequently rides the bus. If on your way to making a fortune you rent a house, drive a modest car, and limit your daily expenses, know that you are in a good company. Money gives you food, money gives you shelter, money gives you opportunities, if you want to become rich you need to respect money, and you respect money through saving.

Reduce daily expenses

Let's talk about three excellent ways to reduce daily expenses without significantly reducing quality of life: conscious control of expenses, moving to places with low cost of living, and avoiding debt like the plague.

Measure expenses

To limit your daily expenses calculate how much you spend overall and in each major category such as clothing, food, transportation or entertainment. What gets measured tends to improve and if you clearly know how much you spend overall each month and in each major category you will save at least 10% on expenses. Develop a habit of asking yourself "Do I really want to purchase this item for this price?" and you will reduce living expenses without actually reducing quality of life.

Move to places with lower cost of living

Have you ever thought that the cost of living in different places can be significantly different? For example if you work in New York and manage to get the same job with the same salary in Dallas, because of lower taxes and cost of living in this city you will be able to reduce your monthly spending by 50%. But if you are a freelancer living in Dallas and working from home and move to Bucharest, Romania, you will be able to reduce your monthly spending by another 50%. Although it's important to consciously control how much you spend, the biggest savings often come when you move to a different city or even a different country if you are able to maintain the same level of income. Often you can earn the most in places that are most expensive, however if your income doesn't depend very much on location moving to a cheaper city or a cheaper country is an excellent strategy.

Avoid debt like the plague

By default you are free to choose your destiny and move in any direction in your life. You can take risks, you can experiment, you can make mistakes because no matter what happens in life you can easily survive. There are countries where you can live for a couple hundred dollars per month, you can move to a house with your parents or sign up as a volunteer with the Red Cross and travel around the world. Your freedom significantly reduces once you have taken debt for improving life comfort, for example for a house, for a car or education. If you have debt, it's with you for many years and now the purpose of your life becomes not to fulfill your life mission, find the best application of your talents and work in a job you are passionate about, but making sure that you are able to pay off a part of the debt each month. When you take debt you exchange a small improvement of your comfort for your freedom and your bright future. If you want to become rich, avoid debt for improving life comfort like the plague because debt is a kettlebell tied to your leg during a run towards financial success.

Rather go to bed without dinner than to rise in debt – Benjamin Franklin

If you buy things you do not need, soon you will have to sell things you need. – Warren Buffett

There are thousands and thousands of people out there living lives of quiet, screaming desperation who work long, hard hours, at jobs they hate, to enable them to buy things they don't need to impress people they don't like. – Nigel Marsh

Buying a house, a car and education

For the majority of people a house, a car and education are highly emotional purchases that boost self-esteem and give a sense of success. If you say to a stranger: "I have graduated from an Ivy League university, I have a five bedroom house in a prestigious neighborhood, and I drive a luxury car," the stranger would think: "You made it! You are successful." However financial success isn't associated with purchases, it's associated with your ability to increase the difference between income and spending, and ironically the highest savings come from not buying a house, buying a cheap or inexpensive education, and driving a mass market car. Before you decide to buy a house, a car or education read an economic analysis of these purchases below.

Buying a house

Let's consider a real-life case, you have $400,000 and consider purchasing a house in Dallas, where real estate is relatively affordable. Overall cost of living in this house without a cost of purchase within 30 years would include a real estate tax of 2.1% per year, house maintenance cost of 1% per year, and community fee of $350 per month. If we sum these things up, you will spend $498,000 for living in this house for 30 years.

Let's consider an alternative scenario where you rent a similar house for 30 years for $3000 per month. In this case you will spend overall $1,080,000 for living in this house for

30 years. Now we get to the most interesting part, at the beginning of the rental period you invest $400,000 in an S&P 500 Index fund for average 8% after tax interest. Within 30 years you would have earned on interest for your investment $4,025,000.

As you can see in the first scenario you spent $498,000 on living in a house and in the second case you have spent $1,080,000 and earned $4,025,000. So if you decided to purchase a house you would have lost ($4,025,000-1,080,000+498,000) = $3,443,000. As you can see purchasing a house for $400,000 is not an economically wise decision because you may lose $3,443,000. When you rent you also can change rental contracts and always live in houses that are under 10 years of age, avoid broker fees during purchase and sale of the house, easily move to a different city when your career needs it, and have more free time because you do not perform maintenance of the house. Many people buy houses because this purchase makes them feel good and raises their self-esteem, however if you want to become rich quicker make financial decisions not based on emotions but based on factual calculations and rent.

Buying a car

If you buy a new mass market car, for example a Honda Civic, it might cost around $20,000. If you buy a luxury car of a similar size, for example an Audi A5, it might cost around $45,000. Besides a cost that is 2.5 times higher, a luxury car would also have a more expensive car insurance, higher consumption of gas, higher maintenance costs and higher oil change costs. If you are on the way to becoming rich in future it may be more economically wise to purchase a mass market car rather than a luxury car.

Now, let's consider whether it is better to purchase a new or a used mass market car? Imagine that you have purchased a new Honda Civic for $20,000, you used it for 6 years and sold it for $8000. Your cost of using a car was $2000 per year.

Imagine that you purchased a 6-year-old used Honda Civic for $8000, you used it for 6 years and at the age of 12 years you sold it for $2000. Because the car is older certain parts needs to be replaced with time and during each of these 6 years you have spent on average $1000 on maintenance. In this case you have spent ($8000-$2000+6000)/6=$2000 per year on using this car. Although these calculations give just a ballpark estimate you can see that on average per year cost of driving is the same for a new and a used car. However driving a new car has significant benefits: it's more comfortable because it's not yet worn out and also has more technologically advanced engine, transmission and features.

Although a luxury car may give a higher feeling of self-esteem and a used car may seem the cheapest option of transportation, the most economically wise purchase on the way to becoming rich is driving a new mass market car. Of course in cities with developed public transportation you may do well even without a car.

Buying higher education

One of the most expensive purchases that people make is higher education. People dream about their children going to prestigious universities and think that after graduation they will have a higher income than people without higher education. And... they are right, but have you ever thought how much exactly higher education increases income?

According to a U.S Census Bureau 2002 report, over the span of their career (40 years of working time) high school graduates earn $1,200,000, bachelor's degree holders earn $2,100,000 and master's degree holders earn $2,500,000. Now let's calculate from an economic perspective how profitable is a decision to obtain a degree at a prestigious university.

Imagine that you have got accepted to Harvard University where at the moment the total cost of attendance is $70,000 per year. A four-year bachelor's degree would cost $280,000. Now your parents come to you and say: "First option for you is that we pay $280,000 for your education and within 40 years you will earn $2,100,000 according to U.S Census Bureau statistics. Second option is that we invest this $280,000 for you in an S&P 500 Index fund with average return on investment of 8% per year and within 40 years you will have made $6,000,000 doing nothing. You will make your own choice if you want to work or not but even if you don't, you will make 3 times more within these 40 years. Which option do you choose?"

By this I don't want to say that you shouldn't obtain a university degree, I just want to place a seed of doubt in your head of how wise paying for an expensive university degree is from an economic perspective. After talking to hundreds of my students and learning about the impact of education on their careers I came to the conclusion that you should pay for expensive higher education only if a degree gives you a government-issued license necessary for your occupation, for example if you study to become a doctor, a nurse, a pharmacist or a lawyer.

If you intend to work in a job that doesn't require a particular government-issued license such as a software developer, a salesperson or an entrepreneur, it is economically wise to make sure that your education is either cheap or free. For example, if you want to become a software developer instead of Harvard University you may study at the University of Texas at Austin and if you are a Texas resident your cost of attendance would be $25,000, or you may even go one step further and study for free at Ludwig Maximilian University of Munich in Germany spending only $10,000 per year on living expenses. When you come to a job interview an employer would be more interested in your programming experience and knowledge rather than in the title of the university from which you have graduated.

One of the most important steps on the way to becoming rich is increasing the difference between your income and spending so that you have savings for investments. After you have done everything to increase your income, do the following to reduce spending: keep track of how much money you spend in each major category, consider moving to places with a low cost of living, avoid taking debts for increasing comfort, rent an apartment or a house, drive a new mass market car, and acquire a cheap or free higher education if it isn't required for a government license for your occupation. Now that you know how to save money, you will learn how to do the most important step on the way to becoming rich, which is investment of saved money.

How money grows

The Wealth Formula says: (Income – Cost of Living)*(Interest on Investment) = Growing Wealth. The biggest reason why people become rich is that they don't only work themselves, but they also make their money work with them. No matter how talented or hardworking you are, if you invest correctly, your saved money at some point will bring more money than you can earn yourself. Investments are a multiplier of your effort and on the way to becoming financially successful, it's a mandatory tool to use.

Let's imagine that you earn $100,000 per year, you manage to live on $50,000 and every year you invest the remaining $50,000 with 10% interest. Furthermore each year you reinvest the earned interest also at 10% interest. By the end of the first year you will have $50,000, by the end of the second year you will have ($50,000+$50,000*1.1) = $105,000, by the end of the third year you will have ($50,000+$105,000*1.1) = $165,500 and this sequence continues.

At the end of the eighth year you will have $571,000 and from now on even if you stop investing half of your income every year, you will earn over half of your income simply from interest. By the end of the twelfth year you will have $1,069,000 in your account and even if you stopped investing half of your income at this point every year you will earn your entire income simply from interest. If you continue investing $50,000 per year after 30 years you will have $8,224,000. After 40 years you will have $22,129,000. After 50 years before you probably retire you will have $58,195,000, you will be filthy rich although your entire life you could have worked in a simple job like a software developer, a nurse or a truck driver. Now imagine, that when you are already wise and old, you invite your grandson or granddaughter who has recently graduated from college and say: "I will give you my entire wealth, however under one condition." Your grandchild asks: "What condition?" And you say: "If you continue doing what I have started. You will invest every year half of your $100,000 salary with 10% interest in addition to $58,195,000 that I give you."

After 100 years from the day you started investing $50,000 every year with 10% interest, when your grandson or granddaughter is already wise and old, he or she would have $6,889,000,000. Your grandchild would think: "Wow! My grandparent and I weren't business people, we weren't CEOs, we weren't rock stars, we weren't even doctors, but right now I have almost 7 billion dollars and am in the list of the 100 richest people on earth. How awesome is that?"

As you can see, to become rich after you have maximized your income and minimized your cost of living you need to invest the saved money. The invested money begins working for you and through interest creates even more money. Rich people see each dollar as a seed that can be planted to produce dozens of dollars, which after that can be planted and bring thousands. The speed of accumulating wealth depends on what the interest rate is at which you invest money and also for how many years you invest money.

We will discuss how to get the highest interest rate for the lowest risk in the next chapter. The takeaway from this chapter is that people who actually become rich think long term and know that accumulating wealth takes time. As an illustration of how people become rich let's see how one of the richest people in the world with a net worth of $75.6B, Warren Buffett, accumulated wealth.

Warren Buffett started his career as investor at the age of 14, he earned his first $1M at the age of 30 and over 99% of his wealth he accumulated after the age of 53. If you want to become rich fast you will find many con artists who will teach you an expensive lesson that becoming rich fast is close to impossible.

One more tip. Imagine that instead of investing $50,000 at the end of the year with 10% interest you have invested $50,000/12=$4166 at the end of every month when you received a paycheck at 10% per year interest. In this case by the end of the first year instead of $50,000 you would have $52,356. Basically a simple trick of making an investment every month rather than every year allows you to increase the amount of money accumulated in your investment account by 5%. The practice of investing every month rather than every year allows you to increase your future net worth by 5% without risk or additional effort.

Investing saved money is an incredibly powerful tool that can multiply your earning potential numerous times and that is mandatory on the way to financial success. When poor people are children they choose to eat one marshmallow now instead of two in 15 minutes, when they grow up they choose to spend their entire income right now rather than become a millionaire in future. When rich people are children they chose to eat two marshmallows in 15 minutes rather than one marshmallow right now, when they grow up they choose to maximize their income, reduce their spending and invest the difference long term with high interest rate and low risk.

3 Millionaire Factory investment methods

Millionaires rarely have a lot of free cash, they invest the majority of their money to make it work and bring even more money so that their income grows. When you invest money your goal is to have the highest possible return on investment with the lowest risk. Out of thousands of investment methods there are three that have the best return on investment to risk ratio. You can invest in your own business that you understand and control, you can invest in an S&P 500 Index fund and you can run all purchases through a credit card with cash back. After you realize that these three investment methods are the most effective ones out of all options, you will free your mind from thinking of how to make your saved money grow, and will be able to devote your entire time and energy to reaching new heights in career or business.

The best investment is entrepreneurship

Perhaps the most common way people become rich is through creation of their own business. Let's imagine that a company is a black box that receives money on input and in a year returns the invested sum together with interest. How much return on investment do you think a successful company can give?

In 2017 Apple sales were $217.5B and profits were $45.2B. As a result the profit margin (profits divided by sales) was

45.2B/217.5B=20.7%. Basically if Apple has been your company and you have invested $100 in it, by the end of the year you could earn $20.7. For comparison the same year the profit margin for AT&T was 7.9%, for General Electric 8.3%, for ExxonMobil 3.9%, for Samsung Electronics 11%, for Procter & Gamble 14.5%. According to *Forbes* magazine the average profit margin among the top 20 companies in the world was 14.7% and the average profit margin among top 100 companies in the world was 12.2%. These statistics show that if you have built a large and successful company and on average for many years it gives you a 15% return on investment, than this is an incredible result.

A founder of Berkshire Hathaway, the second richest man in the world and one of the most successful investors of all time, Warren Buffett managed to maintain an average return on investment of 20% for 50 years between 1965 and 2015. History hasn't seen another investor who could maintain a return on investment that high for that long and because many people consider this result a miracle they call Warren Buffett the Oracle from Omaha.

Taking into account these numbers you can see that for a large business 5% return on investment maintained over many years is OK, 12.2% return on investment is great, and 20% is amazing. Having this information you can easily compare these numbers with any investment opportunity that comes your way. If someone ever says to you: "Hey, I know a great thing that can bring you over 20% of return on investment long term and with low risk," then you can easily make a conclusion that it is a scam. Why? Because if it weren't a scam all companies in the world would shut down and people would invest their hard-earned money only in this "incredible" opportunity because it gives higher return on investment.

When you create a small startup and it becomes successful, for the first several years you can have return on investment not only higher than 20%, but even higher than 100% or even 1000% per year. But it is significantly easier to make a return on investment of 1000% per year on a company that makes $1000 in sales, than it is to make 15% return on investment for a company that makes $1B in sales. The risks of a small startup are higher than for a large company and although a small startup might generate incredible growth during the first years it can also easily go bankrupt during the first years. If after ten years of rapid growth your company returns 15% on investment in subsequent years, then you have created an incredible machine for producing money.

When you choose an investment option you need to look at return on investment and risk. If you create a company that becomes successful you will be able to invest the difference between income and spending back into the company and it will give you the return on investment that is higher than any other option. If you create a business that is based on your passion and talents and is aimed to create value for other people, then it will have a significant competitive advantage and risk will be minimized. Investing money in a business that is based on your strengths provides the highest possible return on investment with the lowest risk. The majority of people who built fortunes from scratch have achieved this through entrepreneurship.

Invest in S&P 500 Index fund

The stocks of U.S. companies in long-term perspective return on investment 10% per year rather consistently and this trend has been maintained for over 100 years. They grow because of technology progress, because of the U.S. economy and population growth, and because companies aim to create even more value for society. You as investor need to understand that in each particular year companies have different performance, some companies have enormous growth, some stagnate and some have losses, however the stock market overall on average gives a return on investment of 10% per year.

Standard & Poor's 500 Index (the S&P 500) was created in 1926. It is calculated based on stocks of the 500 largest corporations in the USA and is weighted by the value of their market capitalization. Every year the list of the biggest 500 companies that represent over 80% of the market value of all U.S. stocks and an S&P Index is updated by Standard & Poor's Index Committee. Between 1931 and 2006 the average annual return on the Total Stock Market Index was 10.2% and an average annual return on the S&P 500 Index was 10.4%. As you can see S&P 500 matches very closely the total USA stock market and if you invest in S&P 500 it's similar to purchasing a stock not of a particular company but a stock of the entire USA stock market.

After investing in your own company, the S&P 500 Index fund is the best investment option. Let's discuss the benefits of this investment option that make the S&P 500 Index a standard to which all other investment options are compared:

Firstly S&P 500 Index provides an incredibly high return on investment that is on average approximately 10% per year. Just think about it, for a company to have a return on investment that is 15% is a great result, but it involves a lot of your time and effort. But S&P 500 Index fund has a return on investment on average 10% and is completely passive, which means that you don't have to do anything at all after the money is invested.

Secondly investing in S&P 500 has a relatively low risk. S&P 500 index eliminates individual stock risk, market sector risk and manager selection risk and only a stock market risk remains. Because of stock market volatility, the short-term performance of S&P 500 Index is unpredictable: for example, in the 1990s S&P 500 return on investment was awesome, but in the 1930s it was terrible. What is important to understand is that long-term S&P 500 Index return on investment is rather consistent.

According to recent statistics, the probability that in any given year you will lose money with S&P 500 Index fund and have a negative return on investment is 32%. The probability of having a negative return on investment over a 5-year period drops to 13% and over a 10-year period drops to 2%. There has never been a 15-year period in history when S&P 500 Index fund had a negative return on investment and lost money. This means that if you aim to invest in S&P 500 Index fund for a long-term perspective, the stock market volatility risk will be reduced and you will earn 10% annual return on investment over the period of investment with a very high probability.

Finally S&P 500 Index fund is a very low cost-investment option, meaning that you will have to give away the smallest portion of your income in the form of investment fees and government taxes. For example from the sum of your investment in S&P 500 Index fund you will have to pay approximately 0.15% per year to the company through which you make an investment, and if you invest for periods of time longer than one year you will pay up to 20% in taxes on your income. Alternatively if you have invested in a mutual fund, a hedge fund or a venture capital fund you might pay at least 3% to the company through which you make an investment and up to 39.6% in taxes on your income. As you can see from the cost perspective, S&P 500 Index fund is an excellent option. (For simplicity of tax calculations everywhere in this book are used maximum short-term and long-term capital gains taxes in 2017.)

In summary, investing in S&P 500 Index fund is a second-best option after investing in your own business. This investment option provides an excellent average annual return on investment of 10%, which even many big companies fail to provide. It also provides relatively low risk compared to other investment options because it eliminates individual stock risk, market sector risk and manager selection risk with only market risk remaining that can be reduced by long-term investment. Also S&P 500 Index fund allows you to give away the least part of your income because of the very low investment company fees and reduced taxes. In further chapters you will see why S&P 500 Index is better than many other popular investment options such as becoming a stock trader, venture capital firms, hedge funds, mutual funds, real estate and bonds.

Credit card is a knife

Credit cards aren't actually an investment option, but they are an excellent way to make money grow. You can open a credit card in a bank with 2% cash back on all purchases, which means than when you purchase any good or service with a credit card you get 2% of this money back as a bonus from the bank. Think about it, you can get 2% on all money you spend, without any work or risk. For example if you spend $100,000 per year and run all your purchases through the credit card you can get $2000 in cash back.

Now let's consider a real-life case. You are self-employed or have a small business that sells products for $200,000 per year. You have spent $100,000 on advertisements or on product creation, and earned $100,000 in profits. From $100,000 in profits you paid 30% in taxes which leaves you with $70,000 in disposable income. Here is a trick: You run through your credit card not only all your personal purchases for $70,000 but also all business-related purchases for $100,000. As a result you have earned $170,000*0.02 = $3400 in cash back. Using a credit card allowed you to increase your disposable income by $3400/70,000 = 4.8% without any risk or work.

Credit cards are an incredible tool that can increase your disposable income by 2% or 5%, however like a knife it has both a positive application and a negative application. A knife can help you to prepare a salad, but a knife can also help you to kill yourself. The same is true with a credit card, if you use it just for cash back purposes you can earn free money, but if you use it to purchase goods that you can't afford you will get the most expensive loan in the world. If you don't pay a credit card balance on time you will pay up to 25% APR in interest, which make you lose much more money than you earned.

A credit card is an incredible tool for increasing your income by several percent without risk. However remember that a credit card for a rich person is only a tool to earn cash back and improve credit history. You always have to pay the balance on a credit card by the end of the month from your main account to avoid paying enormous interest as a fine.

There are the three best options for making your money grow and often people who become rich use all of them. You can invest saved money either in your own business or in S&P 500 Index fund and use a credit card for cash back. Once you make a firm decision in what you will invest your money, you will free your mind, reduce investment-related stress, and be able to concentrate 100% of your effort on your career as an employee or entrepreneur. This decision will make your own life better, will make lives of other people better and will significantly increase your speed of accumulating wealth.

Never depend on a single income. Make investment to create a second source. – Warren Buffet

Most investors, both institutional and individual, will find that the best way to own common stocks is through an index fund that charges minimal fees. Those following this path are sure to beat the net results (after fees and expenses) delivered by the great majority of investment professionals. – Warren Buffett

The shortest route to top quartile performance is to be in the bottom quartile of expenses. – Jack Bogle

By periodically investing in an index fund, the know-nothing investor can actually out-perform most investment professionals. — Warren Buffett

A low-cost index fund is the most sensible equity investment for the great majority of investors. My mentor, Ben Graham took this position many years ago and everything I have seen since convinces me of its truth. — Warren Buffett

Laws of investing

There are numerous financial companies and financial consultants who are eager to help you with investment of money. You may think: "These people have excellent education and many years of experience. They may know much better than I how to invest my money." The problem is that you may either receive bad service or lose money with such an approach, because there is no historical evidence of superior stock-picking skills among investment experts. In this section you will learn three fundamental laws of investment that are true in all cases and knowing which you will be able to make more effective investment decisions than the majority of investment experts with financial education and years of experience.

Past performance doesn't predict future returns

In the 1970s, the 44 Wall Street Fund managed by David Baker Jr. was the top-performing U.S. diversified stock fund and attracted thousands of eager investors that learned about its past results. Unfortunately for people who thought: "Well, if the fund performed well in the past, it should perform well in future," 44 Wall Street Fund became the worst-performing mutual fund during the 1980s.

Burns Advisory tracked performance of 248 stock funds rated 5-star by Morningstar (an investment research firm that ranks funds by past performance) on December 31, 1999. In a decade only 4 out of these funds were still ranked 5-star, 87 ceased to exist and others were downgraded to under 3 stars.

According to the S&P Persistence Scorecard out of 641 U.S. equity funds that were in the top quartile in 2014, only 7.33% managed to stay in the top quartile two years after.

According to research by Gregory Baer and Gary Gensler, authors of the book *The Great Mutual Fund Trap*, out of fifty top-performing funds in 2000, not a single one had been a top-performing fund in 1999 or 1998.

According to research by William Bernstein, author of *Four Pillars of Investing*, for 20 years between 1970 and 1989 the best-performing stocks on the market were Japanese stocks, U.S. small stocks and gold stocks. During the next decade these stocks had the worst performance on the market.

When you want to hire an employee for your company you look at past performance of the candidate because past performance does correlate with future performance. If you want to choose a mutual fund, a stock or a financial adviser to help you to increase return on investment, though, looking at their past performance doesn't make any sense. According to numerous studies, past performance of a stock, a fund or a financial adviser can't by any means predict future returns. Investors are so often fooled by startling past performance of mutual funds, which actually has absolutely no correlation with future performance, that the government requires mutual funds to write in their ads "Past performance is no guarantee of future results," the same as it requires cigarette brands to write "Smoking kills" on every cigarette pack. The first axiom of investing says that if you invest in a stock or mutual fund or hire a financial adviser, their recent successful performance doesn't increase their chances for being successful in future.

There is simply no way under the sun to forecast a fund's future returns based on its past record. – John Bogle

Buying funds based purely on their past performance is one of the stupidest things an investor can do. – Jason Zweig

Market timing isn't possible

You might hear people sometimes say: "If only I had invested money in Google stocks in 2004 I would be a millionaire." "If only I could become a Facebook early investor, I would be a billionaire now." or "If only I had purchased Amazon stock when it went public I would be insanely rich now." When people attempt to predict when exactly to buy a stock and when to sell it to make money, it is called market timing. The only problem in this is that all people are terrible in predicting the future and that market timing isn't possible.

If you would like to predict if a stock will go up or down you will find many trainings, newsletters, books, financial TV programs, and stock market indicators, however unfortunately these all can't help in any way to time the market. In the best case you will spend countless hours learning absolutely useless theories and in the worst case you will lose thousands of dollars on con artists that will promise you help in predicting the future of stocks, however in reality they will make you learn the second law of investing that says: "Predicting stock behavior in short term isn't possible."

In a comprehensive study John Graham from the University of Utah and Campbell Harvey from Duke University tracked

15,000 stock predictions made by 237 market-timing newsletters from June 1980 to December 1992. By the end of the period 94.5% of newsletters went out of business with the average lifespan of just four years. The study concluded, "There is no evidence that newsletters can time the market."

Let's face it, if anybody had the faintest idea of how to time the market, he or she would easily become the richest person in the world and would never share this information. The equity market is affected by a million different factors including investors' emotions and is very random in a short period of time. One of the most respected people in the financial world and a founder of Vanguard investment management company, John Bogle, wrote: "The idea that a bell rings to signal when investors should get into or out of the stock market is simply not credible. After 50 years in this business I do not know of anybody who has done it successfully and consistently. I don't even know anybody who knows anybody who has done it successfully and consistently." One of the most successful investors of all times, Warren Buffett, said: "I never have the faintest idea what the stock market is going to do in the next six months, or the next year, or the next two."

Every year people are trying to find a secret formula that will allow them to predict the future of stock prices, however it's a futile effort, because it contradicts the second law of investing that says: "Market timing isn't possible." These people are no different from gamblers who are playing roulette in a Las Vegas casino who know that by the theory of probability they will lose all their money, but still hope that they will beat math science and win.

If I have noticed anything over these 60 years on Wall Street, it is that people do not succeed in forecasting what's going to happen to the stock market. — Benjamin Graham

The market timer's Hall of Fame is an empty room. — Jane Bryant Quinn

Believing in the ability of market timers is the equivalent of believing astrologers can predict the future. — Larry Swedroe

Passive investors win

There are active investors, who watch financial news, learn different investment methods, spend many hours monitoring their investments, buy and sell stocks all the time. There are also passive investors who invested their money once, and after that sit on a couch and do nothing with their investments for years. By statistics passive investors earn significantly more.

Brad Barber from University of California, Davis and Terrance Odean from University of California, Berkeley conducted a study of 65,000 investors between 1991 and 1996 to learn how trading frequency affected returns on investment. The researchers found that over this period most active traders with 258% annual turnover on their portfolio earned 11.4% per year, average traders with 76% annual turnover earned 16.4% per year, and buy and hold traders with 2% annual turnover earned 18.5% per year. As you can see, passive investors outperformed active investors by 7.1%. By the way for comparison during this period the average S&P 500 Index fund return on investment was 18.34% per year.

Here is what investment experts say regarding the buy and hold investment strategy:

Buy and hold is a very dull strategy. It has only one little advantage – it works, very profitably and very consistently. – Frank Armstrong

Simple buy-and-hold index investing is one of the best, most efficient ways to grow your money to the ultimate goal of financial freedom. – Michael LeBoeuf

Don't trade in and out of funds. Stay invested. Not only does buy-and-hold investing offer better returns, but it's also less work. – Eric Tyson

For investors as a whole, returns decrease as motion increases. – Warren Buffett

Two biggest problems that make active trading significantly underperform passive investments are costs associated with trading and a high tax on short-term capital gain.

Firstly whenever you purchase stocks or sell stocks you have to pay a broker commission for a transaction no matter if you earn or lose money. Secondly when you invest money in a professional company that will invest money on your behalf such as a mutual fund, a hedge fund or a venture capital company you will pay them a management fee, performance fee and numerous other fees that may add up to at least 3% per year. Finally, if your investment is actively managed it can't be qualified for reduced long-term capital gain tax of 20% and is subject to regular income tax of 39.6%.

Let's consider the following case: You have invested $100,000 in an actively managed mutual fund, a hedge fund or a venture capital firm that brought you 10% of return on investment by the end of the year. Out of this 10% you will have to pay 3% in fees to the company that manages your investment which leaves you with 7% return on investment. From this $7000 you will have to pay 39.6% of short-term capital gain tax which leaves you with $4228. So although an investment company said that it brought you 10% return on investment you are able to put only 4.2% in your pocket.

Let's consider an alternative case: You have invested $100,000 in a buy and hold S&P 500 Index fund and did nothing for a year. By the end of the year the S&P 500 Index fund brought you 10% in return on investment. Because you owned stocks for over a year you are qualified for a reduced long-term capital gain tax of 20%. So although a fund brought you 10% in return on investment you can put in your pocket 8%.

As you can see from this example even when a mutual fund, a hedge fund or a venture capital fund had the same return on investment as an S&P 500 Index fund you earned two times less income. However take into account that it is a very rare case when a mutual fund, a hedge fund or a venture capital firm bring the same return on investment as an S&P 500 Index fund, often they bring significantly less.

In 2007 Warren Buffett challenged any investor to select a fund of hedge funds that would beat the S&P 500 Index fund over a period of ten years. Only Ted Seides, a former co-manager of Protégé Partners, took the bet and handpicked a group of hedge funds that he thought would outperform the S&P 500 Index. By the end of 2016, the fund of hedge funds picked by Ted Seides earned approximately 22% after management fees, and S&P 500 Index returned 85%. In fact the fund of hedge funds had returned about 55% return on investment before management fees were extracted, however management fees ate up 60% of the gross return leaving only

22% for investors. In his post on *Bloomberg* Ted Seides wrote: "For all intents and purposes, the game is over. I lost."

As you can see because of high management fees and taxes active investors earn on average significantly less than passive investors. The third axiom of investment says: "Buy and hold passive investment strategy is more profitable than active investment strategy."

When you invest money you need to avoid by all means all "middlemen" such as: brokers, money managers, investment coaches or financial advisers. These middlemen get their chunk from your money no matter if you win or lose and on average as a group earn about $400 billion each year from investors. If you are a passive investor, you will save money on "financial assistants" and taxes and will get a significantly higher return on investment. Be active in your business, be active in your career however not in your investments.

Only buy something that you'd be perfect happy to hold if the market shut down for 10 years. – Warren Buffett.

Of all the expenses investors pay, taxes have the potential for taking the biggest bite out of total returns. – Michael LeBoeuf

If you find investing exciting you are doing it wrong. – Anonymous (unknown source)

Mutual funds and hedge funds

Many people who want to invest their money with maximum return on investment choose either mutual funds or hedge funds. They think: "These guys are professional investors, they have financial education, years of experience and they will make much better decisions of what to invest my money into than I can." After that they evaluate past performance of the funds for the last 3, 5 and 10 years on a statistical service like Morningstar and invest their money in funds that are rated 4 or 5 stars. They think: "If a fund could bring such an incredible return on investment over the last 10 years, then it will likely bring excellent return on investment over the next 10 years."

Let's return back to the weekend that I spent with my friend Jason, who is a serial entrepreneur and a billionaire, and Adam, who worked for many years as an equity fund manager on Wall Street. At the breakfast on Sunday Adam explained why it's a very, very, very bad idea to invest in funds with excellent past return on investment.

Adam said: "Andrii, imagine that in a magical country Randomland at the beginning of the year there are 1024 investment managers who manage small funds by randomly investing money in various stocks. By the end of each year 50% of them have above average performance and 50% have below average performance. Let's follow the top performers who consistently generate excellent results: By the end of the first year 512 investment managers had above average performance, by the end of the second year 256 managers out of these 512 managers had above average performance, by the end of the third year 128 managers had above average performance during all previous years, after we continue this sequence after the 10th year there was one manager left who had above average performance during each year of the decade, let's call him Jack. Now the potential investors look at statistics of various investment managers and stumble upon Jack and say: 'Jack had an above average performance for 10 years straight. He is the most successful investment manager of all and I will definitely give him my money for management. It couldn't be just random that he had 10 successful years straight, and he should know something that nobody else knows and use an incredibly successful strategy.' Because of Jack's incredible performance during previous years, a lot of people invested in his fund, which became very big, in hopes of getting a high return on investment in future. Unfortunately for them Jack's success was indeed just a coincidence and his chances for bringing investors above average return on investment in subsequent years is no different than the chances for all other 1023 investment managers.

"In the real world the situation might be even worse, because a number of mutual funds and hedge funds use a practice of starting 'incubator' funds. Basically an investment management company may start a dozen equity funds with small amount of money managed by different managers and see which one of them would become successful in several years. After that an investment management company would heavily begin to advertise the most successful funds, and close the least successful funds hiding the records that they have ever existed. The majority of people believe that past performance has some impact on future performance of the fund and invest large sums of money in funds that were advertised. In a few years when these most successful funds become unsuccessful and investors begin getting their money back from these funds, the mutual fund or a hedge fund simply closes these funds and tries to remove the records that these funds ever existed. Guess what? After that the investment management company begins to heavily advertise new successful funds from the incubator program and the cycle repeats. There is a reason why all investment companies in their prospectus are required by the government to specify the following warning: 'Past performance is no guarantee of future results.' However the majority of people simply ignore it and earn significantly smaller return on investment than they potentially could."

I asked: "Adam, so if mutual funds and hedge funds don't bring consistently a great return on investment, why do so many people invest in them?" He said: "Firstly because people consistently make investment decisions based on previous performance of the funds, and even earning low return on investment doesn't make them understand that previous performance has no correlation with future results. Secondly because funds spend billions of dollars on advertisements, which are just a small portion of what they earn in management fees and performance fees from investors."

John Bogle, the founder of the Vanguard Group, in his research has analyzed 355 equity funds that existed in 1970 and their performance in the subsequent 35 years. Interestingly by 2005, 223 of these funds had gone out of business due to various reasons. Out of the remaining 132 funds, 108 funds provided return on investment that was equivalent or worse than S&P 500 Index fund. Out of 24 funds that showed better results than S&P 500 Index fund, 15 funds showed results better by 1%, 7 funds by 2% and only 2 funds by 4% or more. If we take into account that with funds you have to pay at least 3% in various fees we can come to the conclusion that out of 355 funds over 35 years a maximum of 2 funds could have outperformed S&P 500 by a little bit. Also you can see from my conversation with Adam it's likely that these 2 funds had their best years at the beginning of the 35-year period and when their success became noticeable and they attracted money from investors, their performance dropped and wasn't as impressive during the subsequent years. Because past performance doesn't guarantee future returns according to the first law of investment the probability that performance of these 2 funds would be as good during the next 35 years after 2005 is extremely low.

Remember the example from the "Passive investors win" chapter where it was shown that if a mutual fund or a hedge fund returns 10% of return on investment you will be able to put 4.2% in your pocket, however if an S&P 500 Index fund returns 10% you will be able to put 8% in your pocket? If you invest in a mutual fund you may have to pay different fees that may add up to 3% in annual fees. With hedge funds it might be even worse and you may pay about 4% in annual fees. (A 2/20 system is common where you pay annually 2% of your investment in management fee and also 20% from the return on investment in performance fee.) According to the USA tax system if you owned a stock for over a year you will pay maximum 20% in long-term capital gain tax, however if the fund actively speculates stocks and owns them for less than a year you will be subject to a regular 39.6% short-term capital gain tax. The increased taxes and fund fees make the generated income for investors significantly lower than income from a buy and hold index fund.

The conclusion from my conversation with Adam and John Bogle's research is the following: taking into account mutual fund and hedge fund fees and high short-term capital gain taxes, over the long term, say 50 years, the probability that a particular fund would provide better average after tax return on investment than an S&P 500 Index fund is close to zero.

With returns corrected for survivorship bias, the average actively managed funds trail the market by about 3 percentage points a year. – Gregory A. Baer and Gary Censel

So much attention is paid to which funds are at the head of the pack today that most people lose sight of the fact that, over longer time periods, index funds beat the vast majority of their actively managed peers. – Paul Farrell

The Greatest Enemies of the Equity investor are Expenses and Emotions. – Warren Buffett

Common ineffective investment methods

Real estate

If you are interested in becoming rich you might stumble upon many articles, books and seminars of "investment gurus" who teach how to become a millionaire by investing in real estate. People often think that investing in real estate is profitable because the prices for houses always grow. Below you will see some research data showing that investing in real estate in long-term perspective is a bad idea.

Firstly according to research conducted by Yale University economist and Nobel Prize winner Robert Schiller the return on residential real estate between 1890 and 1990 was about zero after inflation and since the average annual inflation during the last century was 3.2% this return on investment was low.

Secondly, I have conducted my own research based on an average prices of new houses sold in the USA between January 1985 and January 2015. During this period there was one of the biggest growths in the real estate market in history. At the beginning of this period an average new house price was $82,500 and at the end $292,000, which means that during this time the average annual price increase was 4.3%. Take into account that if you invested in a house in 1985 and sold it in 2015, 4.3% wouldn't be your actual return on investment. Why? Because you generally will pay broker fees during purchase and sale of the house, you will spend maintenance fees to make your house look like new, during the entire time that you own the house you will pay real estate tax and possibly a community fee, and at the time when you sell a house you will pay 39.6% income tax on the difference between purchase and sale price.

As you can see from the data above, buying real estate as a form of money investment is significantly less profitable than investing in stocks and this method of investment isn't recommended in The Millionaire Factory system. If prices for real estate could grow by at least 10% per year long term then nobody would be able to afford buying houses, because they would cost a fortune.

Venture capital funds

Many people think: "How awesome would it be if I had created Google?" And others think: "It would be even more awesome if I could have met Google founders Sergey Brin and Larry Page in 1998 and invested money in their startup. In this case I could have received a share of the company and become a billionaire even without working myself." The only problem with such an approach is that people are really bad at predicting the future and identifying which startups will become successful.

Venture capital funds professionally invest money in startups by performing due diligence of the startup, interviews with founders, and market analysis. Venture capital funds are often managed by former entrepreneurs, who have created successful companies themselves and supposedly can identify startups that will grow rapidly after investment with higher probability than an average investor. The only problem with this scheme is that people very, very, very badly can predict the future, even the venture capital fund managers.

One of the most successful venture capital funds of all times is Sequoia Capital, because it was the early investor in many incredibly successful IT companies such as: Airbnb, Google, Cisco, YouTube, WhatsApp, Apple, Instagram, Yahoo, Oracle, Nvidia and Dropbox. Sounds impressive, right? However take into account that although venture capital firms invest in highly successful companies, they also often invest in startups that fail. Nobody can predict the future in all cases and the success of the venture fund depends on its percentage of successful predictions.

Let's see how much return on investment you could potentially get by investing money into a venture capital firm with the example of Sequoia Capital. Sequoia Capital has invested in many startups in Silicon Valley that eventually became billion-dollar companies and is primarily focused on investing in a rapidly growing IT market which makes it one of the most successful venture capital funds in the world.

According to Sequoia Capital's website the fund's return on investment since its inception in 1970 was 13.65% where S&P Index fund return on investment since 1970 was 11%. Over last 10 years average return on investment for Sequoia Capital fund was 7.05% versus 8.50% for S&P 500 Index fund, and for the last 5 years the return of investment for Sequoia Capital fund was 8.44% versus 15.79% for S&P 500.

Taking this data into account the only figure that might be in favor of Sequoia Capital is 13.65% of return of investment since inception in 1970 which is higher than 11% for S&P 500 over this period. Let's take a look at these figures.

Firstly from 13.65% return on investment you will have to pay at least 3% in various fund fees. That leaves you with 10.65%, and from this 10.65% you will have to pay income tax of 39.6%, so that you can put into your pocket only 6.43%. From 11% of return on investment from S&P 500 Index fund you will pay only short-term capital gain tax that is 20%, so that you can put in your pocket 8.8% which is significantly more than 6.43%.

Secondly, you can't expect realistically 13.65% for future performance, because since inception of the fund there was also a dot com boom period between 1990 and 2000 during which IT stock prices grew abnormally fast and this boom might never repeat again. To more realistically compare long-term future performance of Sequoia Capital and S&P 500 Index fund it's more reasonable to compare the last 10 years during which Sequoia Capital brought 7.05% versus 8.50% from S&P 500 Index. As you can see S&P 500 Index fund brought more and taking into account that from return on investment of a venture capital fund you should also subtract fund-related fees and a high income tax, then S&P 500 Index fund brought significantly more.

Although saying that you are a startup investor may sound even cooler than saying that you are an entrepreneur, investing in venture capital funds is less profitable than investing in S&P 500 Index fund and hence isn't recommended in The Millionaire Factory system. Also don't try to learn investing in startups yourself, you definitely won't be able to do that more successfully than professional investment managers from Sequoia Capital. Focus your time on a business or job that you have passion and talent for and invest the saved money either in growing your primary source of income or in S&P 500 Index fund.

Bonds

Imagine that in 1995 you learned that S&P 500 Index fund has brought 37.58% return on investment. In 1996 S&P 500 Index fund brought 22.96%, in 1997 33.36%, in 1998 28.58% and in 1999 21.04%. Also at the end of 1999 you heard numerous financial analysts saying that the market will continue to grow and if you invest money in S&P 500 Index fund you will make a lot of money. At the end of 1999 you invested $1M, everything that you have earned throughout your life, in S&P 500 Index fund in hopes of becoming rich fast. In 2000 S&P 500 Index fund brought a negative -9.1% return on investment and you thought: "It's frustrating, it's painful, but I hope that the return on investment will be better next year." In 2001 the return on investment was -11.89% and you thought: "I am losing my hard-earned money quickly. I am angry, I am sad, but hopefully the return will be better the next year." In 2002 the return on investment of S&P 500 Index fund was -22.1%, also many financial analysts said that the economy was doing poorly and that stock prices would continue to go down. You thought: "I am getting all my money back from S&P 500 Index fund to save at least the remaining part of my original capital. I can't tolerate these terrible losses anymore." Guess what? In 2003 the return on investment for S&P 500 Index fund was 28.68%.

One of the biggest enemies of any investor is emotions. People tend to buy stocks when prices are high and sell when prices are low, however often price growth is followed by decline and price decline is followed by growth. As you have learned from the previous chapters market timing isn't possible and instead of trying to predict the direction of stock prices it's more reasonable to ignore short-term fluctuation of stock prices and invest long-term to make sure that market fluctuation risks are reduced.

As you can see from the above example it may be a very daunting experience to watch how your hard-earned savings are experiencing losses for 3 years straight. That's why besides return on investment, another important factor is volatility. Imagine that the first investment option gives you a 10% annual average return over 30 years, however during some years you lose up to 40% of your money, and a second option gives you also 10% of annual return, however in the worst year you may lose up to 10% of your money. The second investment option is significantly better because it has volatility of only 10% and will allow you to master emotions more easily during years with loss than the first investment option with 40% volatility.

Perhaps the best investment option for reducing overall volatility of your investment portfolio is bonds. A bond is essentially a loan that you give to a company for a defined period. The company will pay interest on your investment every year, and by the end of the investment period will also return you the original sum of the loan. To reduce risk associated with particular companies it's better to invest in a broad-based investment-grade bond fund such as Vanguard Total Bond Market Index fund, which consists of approximately 6,000 bonds with average duration of five years.

During the 30 years between 1987 and 2016 the average annual return on investment for S&P 500 Index Fund was 11.6% and the worst loss was -37% in 2008. During the same period the average return on investment for Vanguard Total Bond Market Index fund was 6.16% and the worst loss was -2.66% in 1994. As you can see the Total Bond Market Index has a lower average return on investment but also a significantly lower volatility.

The Total Bond Market Index offers a twice lower return on investment in exchange for a low volatility and a good sleep at night. This investment option would be excellent for at least part of your capital for reducing volatility risks if not for one problem – taxes. For all income made with bonds you are subject to regular income tax of up to 39.6%, while for S&P 500 Index fund you are subject to reduced long-term capital gain tax of up to 20%. For the period of 1987 to 2016 from S&P 500 Index fund average 11.6% return of investment you will be able to put in your pocket 9.28% after tax, however from Total Bond Market Index fund average 6.16% return you will be able to put in your pocket only 3.72% after tax. Nevertheless the Total Bond Market Index fund has a very small volatility, but because it's after-tax return on investment is almost 2.5 times lower than return on investment from S&P 500 Index fund this investment option isn't recommended in The Millionaire Factory system.

Future predictors and a gambling gene

One of my students, Jack, graduated from a prestigious university with a major in math and had never gambled in a casino. He said: "I wonder why people gamble in a casino and lose their money. I am a mathematician, and know that according to the theory of probability in the long term your chances of winning in a casino are close to zero. I would never gamble myself." By the age of 60 when Jack retired, he had worked for twenty years as a vice president in a Fortune 500 IT company and saved a large sum of money. During retirement he decided to become a stock trader and increase his capital through predicting direction of stock prices. He thought: "I have been so successful in the corporate world and understand the IT market really well. I have a PhD in math and am sure than analyzing financial data to predict direction of stocks would be significantly easier than developing a new theorem." During the first 3 years Jack had an excellent return on investment and his investment strategy seemed to be working. Unfortunately after the crisis of 2008 everything went out of hand and within the next five years Jack lost everything. Now Jack sells mobile phones in a small shop to make ends meet and tells his grandchildren a story of how he could have become insanely rich if the crisis of 2008 didn't happen.

In 2010 professor Xiaohui Gao Bakshi from University of Maryland and professor Tse-Chun Lin from University of Hong Kong found that the volume of stocks traded by individual investors on the Taiwan Stock Exchange falls by 6% when the biweekly national lottery in Taiwan has a jackpot of $16M or more. Furthermore, when the Taiwan national lottery was first introduced in 2002, the volume of trading on the Taiwan Stock Exchange, which is dominated by individual rather than institutional investors, dropped by 25%. The researchers made a conclusion that there seems to be a connection between lotteries and stock market investing and that many investors consider investing in stocks as a gambling alternative.

Some people say: "I would never buy a lottery ticket, but sports bets is a completely different game. I have watched football for many years and feel that I can predict which team will win." Some people say: "I would never buy a lottery ticket, I would never make sports bets, but the stock market is a completely different game. I can predict the future of stock prices by analyzing financial data." Other people say: "I would never buy a lottery ticket, I would never make sports bets, I would never speculate on the stock market, but investing in startups is a completely different game, because by performing due diligence I can predict which company will become successful." You need to understand that you, I, and everybody else has a gambling gene, and even if you are smart enough to not play common gambling games there will always be some gambling game with a clever title that you might decide to play, because you will have a feeling that you can predict the future based on information available. The only problem here is that all people are not just bad, but terrible at predicting the future.

The human brain is organized in a way that it tries to find patterns even in random events. Try to flip a coin a hundred times and you will develop a feeling that based on previous results you can predict on which side the coin will fall the next time, even though theoretically the probability of getting heads or tails is equal. Look at the sky and you might see that clouds are organized in the form of hearts, trees or faces although in reality clouds are completely random. When you think that based on previous data you can select a winning lottery ticket, choose a winning sports team or predict a direction of stock prices even though theoretically predicting the future isn't possible, this is called a gambler's fallacy.

In 1913 in Monte Carlo, casino people noticed that at one of the roulette tables black came up 15 times in a row. People thought: "If black came up 15 times in a row, then next time red should definitely come up," and bet their money on red. When black came up again this roulette table attracted even more people who thought: "If black came up 16 times in a row, then next time red should definitely come up" and bet on red. In that Monte Carlo casino on this particular table, black came up eventually 26 times in a row and although it's a very rare event, it happened. People couldn't believe that this sequence happened completely by chance, fell prey to a gambler's fallacy and lost a lot of money.

In 1994 a hedge fund called Long-Term Capital Management (LTCM) was founded with the help of two Nobel Prize winning economists, Myron Scholes and Robert Merton. They believed that they had developed a statistical model that could eliminate risk from investment. The fund attracted many investors because of its intriguing background story and excellent return on investment during the first years of existence. During the first year the return on investment after fees was 21%, during the second year it was 43% and during third year 41%. In 1998, when the fund managed $4.72 billion of investor money and $124.5B of borrowed money, it lost $4.6B due to the 1997 Asian financial crisis and 1998 Russian financial crisis. To prevent negative impact on the economy from the fund's collapse, 14 financial institutions under the supervision of the Federal Reserve did a recapitalization of the fund for $3.6B and in 2000 it was completely liquidated. This was a very expensive lesson to learn that even very smart economists can't predict the future but can fall prey to gambler's fallacy.

People who gamble with lottery tickets, with sports bets or stocks continue gambling even after their predictions don't come true because occasional wins release dopamine which is a hormone of happiness that makes you experience pleasure. Gambling, just like alcohol, drugs or sugar, is an addiction that can make you feel good short term, however in exchange for long-term negative consequences. According to research conducted by the University at Buffalo's Research Institute of Addictions, 82% of individuals in the USA gambled in 2001, and according to data from H2 Gambling Capital, gamblers in the USA lost approximately $116.9B in 2016. As you can see gambling is a widespread problem and is dangerous on your way to financial success, however what is even more dangerous than lotteries, casinos and sports betting is disguised gambling. When you speculate in stocks, trade on Forex, buy shares in startups or jump on a new and shiny opportunity, you may think that your investment is based on a well-thought analysis of data available to you, however in reality you are falling prey to gambler's fallacy.

Professor Philip Tetlock, a psychologist, did a long-term study on expert opinion that began in 1984 when he was at the University of California, Berkeley, and lasted 20 years. Tetlock picked 284 experts that were often invited by mass media to comment on political and economic trends and asked them to assess the probability that various events would or wouldn't happen. For example he asked: "Would there be a nonviolent end to apartheid in South Africa?" "Would Gorbachev be ousted in a coup?" or "Would the United States go to war in the Persian Gulf?" By the end of 2003, the experts had made 82,361 predictions if a subject in question would remain as is, would increase (political freedom, economic growth) or decrease (repressions, recession). It turned out that experts, who have spent decades learning how the world functions and who make a living giving political and economic advice, made less accurate predictions than a dart-throwing monkey who randomly picked each of the potential future outcomes with a 33% probability. People love making and listening to predictions, however consider advice that you hear from experts as a source of entertainment rather than a reliable source of information for investment decisions.

Firstly, remember that a gambling gene is inside every person, and even if you never play roulette in a casino, never buy lottery tickets, and never bet on sports there will always be some disguised gambling game with a smart title like "stock trading," "startup investing" or "buying real estate" that will make you think that you can predict the future based on past data available to you such as news, expert opinions, graphs or technical indicators.

Secondly, remember that our brain is organized in a way that it tries to find logical patterns even in random data, and if you are analyzing historical data long enough, you may inevitably develop a "secret investment strategy" that is supposed to make you richer, but in reality will make you poorer. People are extremely bad at predicting the future and one of the best decisions that you can make on the way to becoming rich is saying honestly to yourself: "I have a gambling gene but I will make sure to not let it affect my investment decisions. Nobody can predict the future correctly including me, so I won't fall prey to a gambler's fallacy and won't even try."

Finally, when investing money, never violate the 3 laws of investing: past performance doesn't predict future returns, market timing isn't possible, passive investors win. If while investing money you are having fun, then most probably you are doing it wrong. You can have fun in your career, in your family, in your hobby but when it comes to investments, make a boring and dispassionate decision to invest money long-term in a stocks index fund.

I'd compare stock pickers to astrologers, but I don't want to badmouth astrologers. – Eugene Fama

Bubbles and public madness

Occasionally in the world so-called bubbles happen when prices of a particular asset grow very rapidly, because more and more people invest in it, and at some point these bubbles burst and prices drop very rapidly because the initial price growth was caused not by intrinsic value of the asset but because of a temporary public madness. Recently the USA experienced the dot com bubble of 2000 and the real estate bubble of 2008, and you can be sure that in the future you will face other bubbles as well. As an investor you need to understand how a bubble is formed and if you should invest money in a fast-growing asset when mass media and people around you are constantly talking about it.

In 1951, social psychologist Solomon Asch conducted an experiment with students of Swarthmore College to research social conformity. Asch placed a student in a group of eight people to participate in a simple "perceptual task." The people in the group were actors trained by Asch, who were introduced to a student as other participants, and the true purpose of the experiment was to test how this subject would react to the actors' behavior. Each student viewed a card with a line on it, followed by another card with three lines labeled "A", "B" and "C," one of which had the same length as the line on the first card, and two other lines that were clearly longer or shorter. Each participant sequentially had to say aloud which line on the second card was equal in length to the line on the first card. The answer on each question was obvious and an average person would answer it correctly with 100% probability. Before an experiment the actors were instructed how to respond to each trial card presentation and were seated in a way that a real participant always responded last. The participants gave their answers during 18 trials with card comparisons. During the first two trials both the test subject and actors gave the obvious correct answer. On the third trial all actors gave the same wrong answer, out of the remaining 15 trials actors gave the same wrong answer in 11 of them. Asch analyzed how the test subjects responded during 12 trials when actors gave the same wrong answer, and this was the purpose of the experiment. Having analyzed many real participants Asch determined that the test subjects stuck to the obvious correct answer in 63.2% of cases, however in 36.8% of cases test subjects ignored the obvious correct answer, thought that the majority of people can't be wrong, and chose the same wrong answer as the actors. As you can see, people have a herd mentality. If even on obvious questions they give a wrong answer in one-third of cases, how do you think they behave during a bubble when a future direction of the market isn't obvious and the majority of people say that real estate or IT stock prices will rapidly grow?

In 1986 economists Robert Schiller and John Pound did a survey to determine how investors are first drawn to a stock that they end up buying. They mailed a questionnaire to a random sample of individual investors asking: "What first drew your attention to the company?" Only 6% specified periodicals or newspapers. The vast majority of the answers named sources that involved interpersonal communication with other people. Even though people read and analyze a lot of data themselves, their investment decisions are heavily influenced by word of mouth recommendations.

Journalists are in the business of attracting audience attention and they are constantly searching for word of mouth worthy stories. During a bubble the news media gets an unlimited source of information to share with the audience. The news media can share an interesting story behind the asset for which the prices are growing, after that it can report changes in prices for the asset on a daily, weekly or monthly basis, finally it can share opinions of various experts about the future of the asset and also success stories of investors who earned a lot of money with this asset. People get startling financial news that is interesting to read or watch, news media gets an excellent source of regular captivating news, and the bubble gets a constant supply of excited investors.

Remember my weekend with Jason, a serial entrepreneur, and Adam, a former Wall Street shark, during which they shared with me their secrets for becoming rich? During our lunch on Sunday, Adam said: "Andrii, let me explain to you how bubbles get created and eventually burst using the example of the dot com bubble. At the beginning the stock prices of IT companies began to grow slightly and after that a little bit faster. The story that we were entering a new era in which the internet would change all areas of life got created to explain this growth. The news media got interested in the story and in stock prices' growth and began releasing updates about IT stock prices first occasionally, then more often and then even more often.

"These news cascades inspired a small number of investors to buy stocks of internet companies, and guess what, within a short period of time they earned excellent return on investment. At this point news media began sharing heavily success stories of investors who made a lot of money with investing in IT startups, which encouraged even more investors to buy stocks of IT companies. Now came into effect the power of word of mouth and people who made great return on investment with stocks of IT companies told about their success to their families and friends. At this point already taxi drivers, nurses, truck drivers, mechanics, teachers, firefighters and housewives, who are very far from the stock market, got excited about a chance to make easy money and purchased stocks of IT companies.

"Unfortunately for them it was already the year 2000 and the supply of excited investors who increased demand for and hence the prices of IT stocks ended. Because the price growth was dictated not by intrinsic value of IT companies, but by public madness, when the stream of excited potential investors ended, the price for IT stocks went a little bit down. The news media began to write that the prices were going down, people began to sell their stocks as a result lowering prices even further, the news media wrote about price reduction even more, now everybody began to talk about how rapidly the prices were going down and tried to sell their stocks. When the dot com bubble burst, many IT companies went bankrupt, the stock prices went down as quickly as they went up and the economy was severely hit. The same mechanism that has blown the dot com bubble quickly has burst the dot com bubble quickly. The mechanism that is based on an intriguing background story, news media and word of mouth blows and bursts any bubble in the same way."

Now that you have learned how the bubbles work you may ask: "Andrii, can I make money by investing during the bubble if I predict when it begins and ends?" I would recommend you ignore all bubbles because market timing isn't possible and nobody can correctly predict when the bubble begins and when it ends. Whoever tries, is simply a gambler. In most cases when you begin hearing about how the prices are growing rapidly for a certain asset from news, from colleagues and from friends, the bubble is already close to bursting. If you want to become a millionaire, ignore the bubbles and ignore public madness – they aren't your game. Spend time and energy on work that you are passionate about and have talent for, and invest money either in your own business or in S&P 500 Index fund. In the long term this strategy will make you rich much faster than trying to chase an animal called "Get rich quick" because this animal doesn't exist.

Those who cannot remember the past are condemned to repeat it. – George Santayana

The Millionaire Factory checklist

By now you have learned The Millionaire Factory system, which if followed precisely will significantly shorten your path to becoming rich. Before you finish reading this book and take actions towards accumulating wealth let's review the main components of The Millionaire Factory system.

1) The Wealth Formula

The Wealth Formula says: (Income – Cost of Living)*(Interest on Investment) = Growing Wealth. In order to become rich you simply need to increase income, reduce cost of living and invest the difference with the highest return on investment and lowest risk. The formula is simple, however to make it work you need to take care of all three components.

2) The Millionaire's Triangle

In order to maximize your income you need to do work that is on the intersection of passion, talent and a goal of creating value for people. If you focus only on work in this intersection, you will have a significant competitive advantage and will have an enormous success either in business or career.

3) Set a long-term goal

One of the biggest differences of people who become rich from people who never do is that they have a long-term goal. Make sure that you have a long-term goal for at least the next decade and this will significantly increase the effectiveness of actions that you take towards becoming rich.

4) Money-making actions

Develop a habit of identifying a golden task that will bring you the biggest value and getting the maximum from a present moment. Years consist of months, months consist of days and days consist of moments. If you make sure that you work with maximum productivity at the present moment, you will make sure that you can do more work within a day, a month or a year than the majority of people could only dream of.

5) Rich brain, poor brain

Life isn't easy and everybody has numerous obstacles on their way to success, however people react differently to them. A poor brain tries to find excuses why a problem can't be solved, and a rich brain is focused on how to solve a problem. If you want to accumulate wealth quickly, you need to use your rich brain much more often than your poor brain.

6) Spend less than you earn

To increase the amount of saved money that you will be able to invest, you need not only increase income, but also decrease cost of living. To reduce daily expenses simply track how much money and on what you spend within a month, because what gets measured gets improved. To save money on the biggest purchases that people make, rent a house, drive a new mass market car and if your education isn't critical for obtaining a government-issued license make sure that it's either cheap or free.

7) 3 Millionaire Factory investment methods

The investment option with best risk to return ratio is investing money in your own business for which you have passion, talent and that is focused on creating value for people. The second investment option is S&P 500 Index fund, which provides excellent return on investment and doesn't require work from your side. The third method for getting extra return on your money is credit cards, if you use them properly you can earn at least 2% cash back on your spending without work from your side and without risk.

8) Reduce taxes and costs of an investment

Remember that when you earn money through an investment option you also need to pay taxes and costs associated with this investment option. When you invest in S&P 500 Index fund long term you may pay no taxes on capital gain for years until you decide to put a profit in your pocket and even at that point you are subject to only up to 20% long-term capital gain tax. If you invest with mutual funds, hedge funds or venture capital funds you may not only have to pay up to 39.6% in income tax but also approximately 3% per year in fund related fees.

9) Don't violate laws of investment

When investing money never violate the 3 laws of investment: Past performance doesn't predict future returns, market timing isn't possible, buy and hold passive investors earn the most. When you try to violate any of these laws your return on investment will diminish.

10) Take control over your gambling gene

Be aware that you have a gambling gene that might make you think that you have the ability to predict the future when investing in stocks, startups or other assets. Take control over your gambling gene and invest using methods that have proved to be extremely effective for many generations of millionaires.

When the majority of people think about being rich, they imagine expensive cars, big houses and private jets. Imagine that you were born without a talent for being an entrepreneur, a rock star or a football player, but your talent is being an excellent math teacher. You might ask yourself: "Either I can fulfill my life purpose and be a teacher or I can try to climb a corporate ladder or start my own business to one day own expensive toys." If you ignore your vocation and try to become rich by any means, most probably your life will not be happy and eventually you won't get rich. In The Millionaire Factory system I want to introduce a new definition of what being rich is that will allow everyone to become rich regardless of their talents, passions and dreams. Don't aim to become a billionaire, don't aim to own expensive cars, big houses and private jets, but aim to maximize your income doing what nature had in mind for you and gaining extra passive income through investments.

If you are a teacher try to become the best teacher you can be and get a job in the best school in town. Because the value you generate for the world increases, your salary will also increase. After that increase the gap between your income and cost of living and invest the difference in S&P 500 Index fund. Also don't forget to use a credit card with 2% cash back whenever you shop. This strategy long term will allow you to earn five times more than an average math teacher and in a social tribe of teachers you will be insanely rich. As a side bonus you will enjoy fulfilling your life purpose and doing the work that you were destined to do. Society will be grateful for your excellent contribution to the world and will say "Thank you" both verbally and in the form of money.

Close your eyes, put your right hand on your heart and ask yourself: "What do I really want to achieve this year?" Now write three specific actions that will get you closer to becoming rich and that you will do within the next 24 hours.

Final words

Several years ago I spent a weekend with my friend Jason, who is a serial entrepreneur and a billionaire and with Adam, who was a successful Wall Street equity manager in the past and currently works as a chef. This meeting has completely changed my understanding of how people become rich and has contributed many interesting concepts to The Millionaire Factory system.

Although this weekend was incredible, it came to an end and after lunch on Sunday my wife, Olena, and I packed our bags, said goodbye to Jason, his wife, Jane, and Adam and were ready to drive to the airport. I looked at Jason and Adam and said: "I just forgot. The Millionaire Factory book would start with me meeting you at this beautiful mansion, I want your words, guys, also to finish it. Please give a final advice that you think is important for my readers to become millionaires."

Adam said: "I'll probably be first. If you realize that the only way to make your money grow is investing in your own business, index funds and using credit cards, you will be able to save a lot of nerves and time for becoming successful in your vocation and maximizing your primary source of income. Don't be excited about your investments, investments should be boring."

Jason, thought, thought again, smiled and said: "If you want to become successful in your vocation and maximize your primary source of income you need to always have a sparkle in your eye. Be excited about your work, work should be fun."

What to read next?

If you liked this book, you will also like *The Business Idea Factory: A World-Class System for Creating Successful Business Ideas*. Principles described in this book will allow you to effectively create successful business ideas and make your life more adventurous.

Another interesting book is *Magic of Impromptu Speaking: Create a Speech That Will Be Remembered for Years in Under 30 Seconds*. In this book, you will learn how to be in the moment, speak without preparation and always find the right words when you need them.

I also highly recommend you to read *Magic of Public Speaking: A Complete System to Become a World Class Speaker*. By using this system, you can unleash your public speaking potential in a very short period of time.

Biography

At the age of 19, Andrii obtained his CCIE (Certified Cisco Internetwork Expert) certification, the most respected certification in the IT world, and became the youngest person in Europe to hold it.

At the age of 23, he joined an MBA program at one of the top 10 MBA schools in the USA as the youngest student in the program, and at the age of 25 he joined Cisco Systems' Head Office as a Product Manager responsible for managing a router which brought in $1 billion in revenue every year.

These and other experiences have taught Andrii that success in any endeavor doesn't as much depend on the amount of experience you have but rather on the processes that you are using. Having dedicated over 10 years to researching behavior of world's most successful people and testing a variety of different techniques, Andrii has uncovered principles that will help you to unleash your potential and fulfill your dreams in a very short period of time.

The Business Idea Factory

A World-Class System for Creating Successful Business Ideas

The Business Idea Factory is an effective and easy-to-use system for creating successful business ideas. It is based on 10 years of research into idea-generation techniques used by the world's best scientists, artists, CEOs, entrepreneurs and innovators. The book is entertaining to read, has plenty of stories and offers bits of wisdom necessary to increase the quantity and quality of ideas that you create multiple times. Once you begin applying strategies described in this book, you will create successful business ideas regularly and make your life more adventurous. You will realize that there are few things that can bring as much joy and success in business as the moment when an excellent idea comes to your head.

Magic of Impromptu Speaking

Create a Speech That Will Be Remembered for Years in Under 30 Seconds

Magic of Impromptu Speaking is a comprehensive, step-by-step system for creating highly effective speeches in under 30 seconds. It is based on research of the most powerful techniques used by winners of impromptu speaking contests, politicians, actors and successful presenters. The book is entertaining to read, has plenty of examples and covers the most effective tools not only from the world of impromptu speaking but also from acting, stand-up comedy, applied psychology and creative thinking.

Once you master the system, you will grow immensely as an impromptu public speaker, become a better storyteller in a circle of friends and be more creative in everyday life. Your audience members will think that what you do on stage after such short preparation is pure magic and will recall some of your speeches many years later.

Magic of Public Speaking

A Complete System to Become a World Class Speaker

The Magic of Public Speaking is a comprehensive step-by-step system for creating highly effective speeches. It is based on research from the top 1000 speakers in the modern world. The techniques you will learn have been tested on hundreds of professional speakers and work! You will receive the exact steps needed to create a speech that will keep your audience on the edge of their seats. The book is easy to follow, entertaining to read and uses many examples from real speeches. This system will make sure that every time you go on stage your speech is an outstanding one.

Made in the
USA
Columbia, SC